# Sue Stratford's
# Knitted Aviary
## A flock of 21 beautiful birds to knit

SEARCH PRESS

# CONTENTS

# INTRODUCTION

I have really enjoyed creating all these little birds. Originally, I was only going to make a robin, blackbird and blue tit. However, I quickly added to these and before I knew it I had a book-full. Everyone has their favourite bird so I was never short of ideas. The Highland Birds (pages 106–117) were a special project I made for Edinburgh Yarn Festival so that visitors would have a souvenir of Scotland to take home with them.

I gathered my designs together and self-published a book called *A Bird in the Hand* with the help of a Kickstarter campaign. It's very exciting that Search Press is now publishing a new book that includes those birds and more, together with ideas for displaying them. At the back of the book is a list of all the people who supported me via the Kickstarter campaign and helped bring the original book to life. I will be eternally grateful to them.

The birds are a great way to learn new techniques and are suitable for beginners and experienced knitters. As you are only working over a small number of stitches, if you do have to take back a few rows, it's not a big deal. Why not challenge yourself and try something new? You'll not only end up having learnt a new technique, but you'll also have a cute bird.

I used tapestry wool to make the birds. As it comes in small quantities, it's ideal, as some of the birds use quite a few colours. The tapestry wools I used are available in more than 400 shades, so I was able to find exactly the colour needed for every bird. Of course, you can knit the birds in whatever thickness of yarn you want – just remember to alter your knitting needle size accordingly. It is best to use needles that are at least two sizes smaller than the recommended size for the yarn you are using, so that your finished knitting is tight and the stuffing does not show through.

The techniques are explained at the front of the book, and there is also a step-by-step tutorial on how to sew the birds together. It is worth spending some time sewing up as this is when the characters of the birds come to life.

Flick forward through the book and you will find ideas for displaying your birds, together with all the instructions to create them. The main thing is to enjoy knitting the birds and to have some fun. Everyone has their favourite bird and you never know – you may end up with a tree full like me!

# MATERIALS & TOOLS

## Yarn

The yarn that I used for these little birdies is tapestry wool. It is perfect for these projects as there is such a wide variety of shades available. There are more than 470 to choose from, so you can match the colours much better than if you use standard knitting yarn.

The yarn is a DK (light worsted/8-ply) weight and pure 100% British wool, which I loved working with. All the birds are knitted flat.

## Knitting needles

You can use whatever knitting needles you like to work these birds. Because they are only small projects, I chose to use double-pointed knitting needles (DPN) as they are shorter than standard needles and work well when you have a small number of stitches. They are also useful for working the i-cord legs for the birds (see page 12).

All the birds are worked using 3mm (US 2 or 3, UK 11) knitting needles, which means that you are working the yarn at a much tighter tension than you normally would. This helps the birds keep their shape when stuffed and prevents the toy filling showing through the stitches.

## Scissors

A small pair of sharp scissors is very useful to keep in your knitting bag. As the birds are only small and you are using more than one colour for a lot of them, you will be reaching for your scissors quite frequently.

## Tapestry needles

I always keep a selection of needles in my bag. Tapestry needles are blunt and therefore less likely to split the yarn when you are sewing up your birds. If you are going to make any of the felt accessories you will also need some sharp embroidery needles with a large eye.

## Felt

You need a small amount of felt for some of the birds (for example the Oystercatcher on page 66 and the Parakeet on page 74). I used a wool felt but you can use any felt that is the right shade. The safety eyes are threaded through the felt and then the felt is trimmed to make a 'ring' around the eye. Turn to page 20 for full instructions on how to do this.

I also use wool felt for all the accessories. It is particularly suitable for the branches and hoops as, if you stretch it, it frays slightly along the edges and looks better than a hard edge.

## Embroidery thread

The embroidery thread is used to hand embroider the leaves and also the detail on the birdhouse. You need a sharp needle with a large eye to go through the felt when using the embroidery thread.

## Chenille sticks

I used a chenille stick for the stem of the tropical flower (see page 134). This allowed me to to position it exactly as I wanted and wind it around the embroidery hoop for the hummingbird (see page 78).

## Toy filling

I always use a polyester toy filling that meets current toy safety standards. It is easy to use and fluffs up nicely to give the birds a bouncy plumpness.

## Pins

Pins are very useful, when making both the birds and the accessories. I pin the bird together before sewing up to ensure I have got the eyes and beak in the right position (see page 21).

## Glue

For the felt accessories I used a strong, all-purpose glue, which dries quickly and also dries clear. The felt is quite firm and so a strong glue is essential. If you are worried that the felt will not stick properly, you can pin it until it sets.

## Blusher

I raided my make-up bag when I was making the felt flowers (see page 132) and used some blusher, which you can apply with a small brush or cotton bud (cotton swab). I love the effect of adding a touch of pink to each flower; it looks very effective and is easy to achieve.

## Erasable marker pen

This pen was an essential part of my kit. It allows you to draw on the felt exactly where you intend to sew. There are different types of erasable pens you can buy. I used one where the ink disappears when you iron the fabric. Check the pen you use for instructions before starting.

Strong, all-purpose glue

Cosmetic blusher

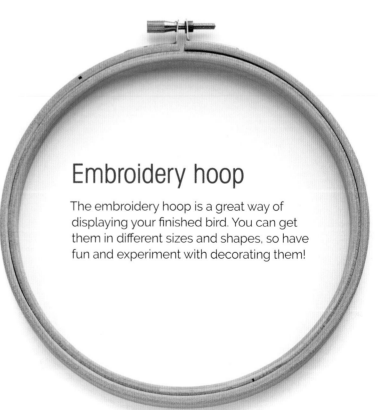

## Embroidery hoop

The embroidery hoop is a great way of displaying your finished bird. You can get them in different sizes and shapes, so have fun and experiment with decorating them!

## Safety eyes

I used safety eyes for the birds in this book. They are easy to fit and are much better than beads, especially if the bird is a gift for a child. I have included a tutorial on how to attach the eyes, which is worth reading before you start (see page 21). However, if your bird will be gifted to a small child, it is better to embroider the eyes using black yarn instead.

# TECHNIQUES

## i-cord

The i-cord technique is a quick and easy way to make a knitted cord that gives the appearance of French knitting. You will need to use double-pointed knitting needles to make them. I have used this technique to knit the birds' legs.

**1** Knit the foot up to the stage where you picked up 2 stitches to make a total of 3 stitches on your needle.

**2** Knit across these 3 stitches.

**3** Slide the stitches to the other end of the needle without turning your work and pull the yarn behind the stitches as shown.

**4** Knit the next row.

**5** Repeat steps 3 and 4 for each row. Pulling the yarn behind the needle means you are working these 3 stitches on a continual 'loop' with no seam to sew up.

# Intarsia

Intarsia is used when you are knitting blocks of different colours. They can be all sorts of shapes or designs, but the difference is that you don't strand the yarn across the back of your work as you do with Fair Isle (see page 14).

**1** Work to where you need to change colour.

**2** Pick up the new colour and cross the old yarn (green) over the new yarn (yellow) and knit the next stitch with the new yarn. Therefore the new yarn 'catches' the old yarn as you start to knit.

**3** Knit the next stitch.

**4** When you reach the next colour change, pick up the green yarn, take it over the top of the yellow yarn and knit the next stitch. Knit to the end of the row.

**5** To work a purl row, pick up the new colour and cross the old yarn (green) over the new yarn (yellow) and purl the next stitch with the new yarn. Therefore the new yarn 'catches' the old yarn as you start to purl.

**6** Purl over the next stitch in yellow.

**7** The finished purled row.

# Fair Isle

This is a method of knitting with two colours in which only a few stitches in the contrasting colour are worked. The yarn not being knitted should be carried at the back of the work and then looped over the working yarn every 4–5 stitches to ensure it stays close to the work. Make sure the loops are loose enough not to pull the work out of shape and distort the knitting, but not so loose that large loops appear at the back of the work. Don't worry too much about the inside of your work, as all the ends of yarn will be inside the bird once you have sewn it up and no one will see them.

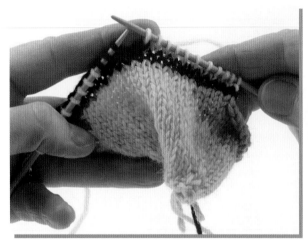

**1** Knit up to the point where you have a colour change.

**2** Pick up the new yarn (black) and bring it underneath the old yarn (cream) to catch it in. Repeat this step every time you change colour.

**3** For a purl row work in the same way. The back will look like this.

**4** If you are working more than 5 stitches in one colour, catch in the yarn you are carrying along the back (black) by looping it over the working yarn.

# Three-needle cast-off

This technique not only gives a really neat finish but means you have one less seam to sew up. You will need a spare needle.

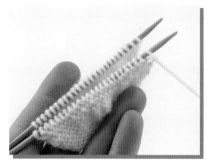

**1** Divide the stitches evenly between two needles.

**2** Fold in half with right sides together. Insert a third needle into the first stitch on each needle.

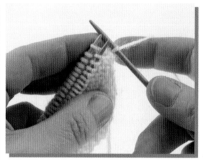

**3** Knit the 2 stitches together.

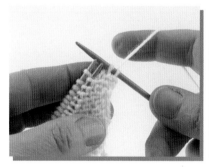

**4** Knit the next 2 stitches together in the same way so you have 2 stitches on the third needle.

**5** Insert the needle into the first stitch and lift it over the second stitch to cast off.

**6** Repeat the process to cast off all stitches and fasten off the last stitch. This shows the finished seam from the wrong side.

The seam viewed from the right side.

# Wrap and turn (w&t)

This technique ensures that you do not end up with a 'hole' in your knitting (see opposite) when working short-row shaping and turning your work mid-row.

## WRAP AND TURN ON A KNIT ROW

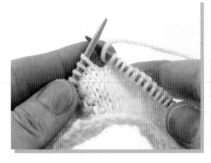

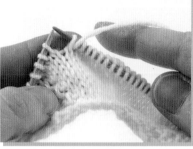

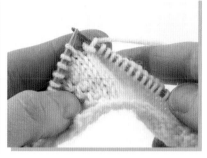

**1** Work to the specified stitch and bring the yarn towards you between the needles.

**2** Slip the stitch on the left-hand needle to the right-hand needle.

**3** Wrap the yarn around the stitch.

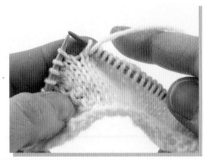

**4** Transfer the stitch back to the left-hand needle. The stitch now has a loop of yarn wrapped around it.

**5** Turn your work and purl the next stitch.

## WORKING THE WRAPPED STITCHES ON A KNIT ROW

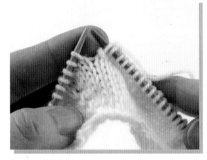

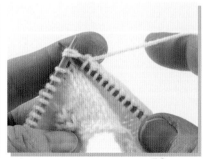

**6** Knit to the wrapped stitch. Without twisting it, slip the wrapped stitch onto the right-hand needle.

**7** Using the left-hand needle, lift the 'wrap'.

**8** Slide the left-hand needle into the wrapped stitch and knit the stitch and the wrap together.

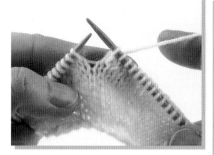

**9** The knitted wrapped stitch.

If you don't use the w&t method, you get holes forming in your knitting, as shown above.

## WRAP AND TURN ON A PURL ROW

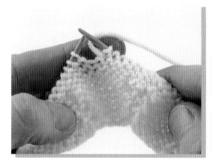

**1** Work to the specified stitch and take the yarn away from you between the needles.

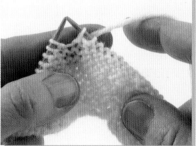

**2** Slip the first stitch on the left-hand needle onto the right-hand needle.

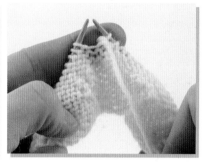

**3** Bring the yarn between the needles and round the slipped stitch.

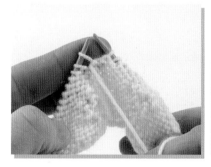

**4** Slide the stitch on the right-hand needle back to the left-hand needle.

**5** Turn your work and knit.

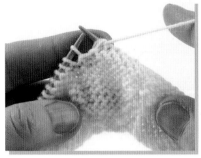 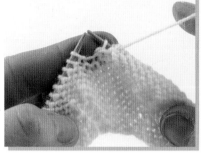 

**6** Purl to the wrapped stitch.

**7** Slip the stitch onto the right-hand needle without twisting it.

**8** Pick up the wrap with the left-hand needle.

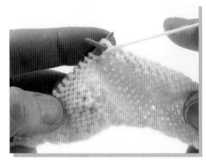 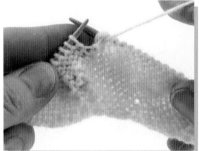

**9** Purl together with the wrapped stitch.

**10** The finished stitch.

# Make 1 stitch (M1)

This useful and easy technique creates an almost invisible increase and I use it all the time. There are other ways of increasing, but this is my favourite.

## MAKE 1 STITCH ON A KNIT ROW

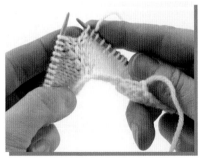 

**1** Knit to where you want to make your extra stitch.

**2** Insert the knitting needles knitwise and pick up the bar between the two needles.

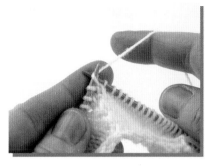 

**3** Slide the resulting loop onto your left-hand needle and knit through the back of the stitch (this tightens the loop) .

**4** The finished stitch.

## MAKE 1 STITCH ON A PURL ROW

 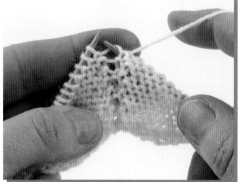

**1** Purl to where you want to make your extra stitch.

**2** Insert the knitting needles purlwise and pick up the bar between the two needles.

 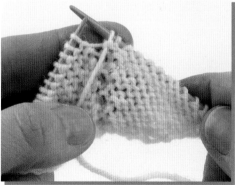

**3** Transfer the bar onto your left-hand needle and purl through the back of the stitch.

**4** The finished stitch.

## ATTACHING FELT BEHIND SAFETY EYES

Some of the birds have a circle of felt behind the safety eyes to add character and make them look more realistic. This is how to do it.

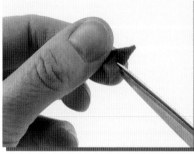

**1** Cut out two 2cm (¾in) squares of felt and have your two safety eyes ready.

**2** Fold each piece of felt in half diagonally and snip a small hole in the centre.

**3** Push the safety eye all the way through the hole.

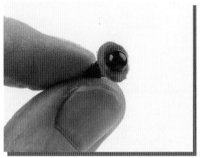

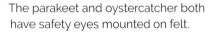

**4** Trim the felt into a circle and the eye is ready to use. See opposite for how to attach the safety eyes.

The parakeet and oystercatcher both have safety eyes mounted on felt.

# Inserting safety eyes and making up

This shows you how to insert the safety eyes and sew up the birds. It might seem very fiddly to stuff the bird, then take the stuffing out to secure the safety eyes, and re-stuff it again, but it makes all the difference with positioning the eyes and beak correctly.

**1** Sew together the seam at the back of the head and along the bird's back, leaving the back of the bird open. Stuff with toy filling and pin the beak in place.

**2** Push a safety eye into the head on either side of the beak, making sure they are evenly positioned.

**3** Remove the beak and the toy stuffing from the head and turn inside out, taking care not to dislodge the eyes.

**4** Push the clear plastic backs onto the eye stalks, making sure they are securely fixed in place.

**5** Turn the bird the right way out and re-stuff the head firmly. Pin the beak back in place and sew on securely using the yarn tail.

**6** To sew up the hole at the bottom of the bird's body, thread the yarn tail through each stitch all around and pull tight to gather and close the hole.

**7** Hide the yarn tail in the body and snip off the end.

# Embroidery

## CHAIN STITCH

Chain stitch can be worked in a straight line or a wavy line if your project requires it.

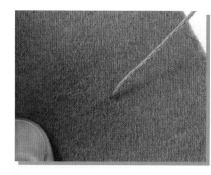

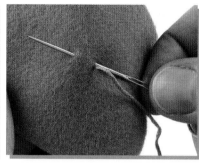

**1** Knot the thread and bring it to the front of your work.

**2** Insert the needle close to where it came up and out again a little further on.

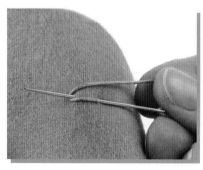

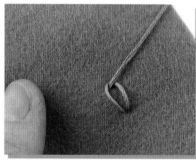

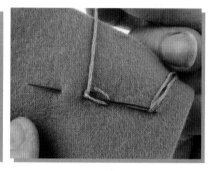

**3** Wrap the thread under the needle.

**4** Pull the needle through and one chain is completed.

**5** For the next chain, push the needle through close to where you last came up.

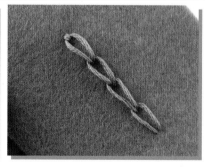

**6** Wrap the thread under the needle again ...

**7** ... and pull through to complete your second chain.

**8** When you have made the required number of chains, push the needle down on the outside of the final chain and fasten off.

# LAZY DAISY STITCH

To make lazy daisy stitch, which is a variation of chain stitch, work up to step 4 opposite for the chain stitch instructions, then continue as below from step 5.

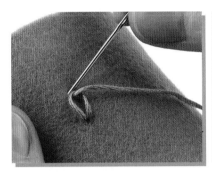

**5** Push the needle down through the felt on the outside of the chain.

**6** This completes the first petal of the daisy.

**7** Make a second chain to the right of the first one.

**8** Continue making chains evenly in a circle until you have made five, which comprise your daisy.

# HINTS & TIPS

## YARN

For birds that are knitted using more than one colour and the Intarsia technique (see page 13), having at least two skeins of tapestry yarn in the same colour enables you to work across the row with one separate strand for each section – making it much easier than winding mini balls of yarn beforehand. When you start, remember to pull the longer thread of yarn you can see and the wool will flow without getting tangled.

The tapestry wool I use has 10m (11yd) on a skein but some brands only have 8m (9yd), so for each pattern the amount required is shown in metres rather than the number of skeins. This will also enable you to work out how much yarn you will need if you are using standard knitting yarn.

The patterns are knitted using 3mm (US 2 or 3, UK 11) knitting needles, unless specified. These needles are smaller than you would normally use with a DK (light worsted/8-ply) yarn. This gives a nice tight finish, stops the toy filling showing through and also prevents the bird from stretching out of shape.

Enjoy making your birds and don't forget to share a photograph on social media (see page 2 for details)!

## COLOURWORK CHARTS

There is colourwork on some of the birds, but it is easy to do and I have used colourwork charts (see below), which makes the instructions much easier to follow. It also helps you to keep your place if you get interrupted in the middle of your project!

The chart headings show which yarn colour you need to use and each line represents a row. The charts are interspersed with the rest of the pattern, so everything is shown in the order in which you knit your bird. Don't worry too much about sewing the yarn ends in; as long as they are secure, you can hide them inside the bird when you sew it up. To help keep your place, use a piece of washi tape or a sticky note.

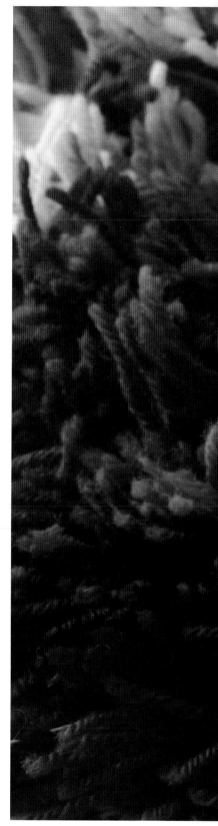

|  | TURQUOISE | ORANGE | TURQUOISE |
|---|---|---|---|
| NEXT ROW: | P3, | P36, | P3. |
| NEXT ROW: | K5, | K32, | K5. |
| NEXT ROW: | P7, | P28, | P7. |
| NEXT ROW: | K8, | K26, | K5, w&t. |
| NEXT ROW: | P6, | P24, | P6, w&t. |

## TENSION

It is worth taking some time to check your tension. To do this, cast on 18 stitches and work 20 rows in stocking (stockinette) stitch. Count 7 stitches in the centre of your swatch and measure. If the section is too big, use a needle that is one size smaller; if it is too small, use a needle that is one size larger. As long as the stitches are nice and tight, the shape of the bird will be good and the toy filling won't show through the work. If you need to carry the yarn across the back of your work, then do! As long as it isn't pulled too tight it will be fine; remember that, once you have sewn your bird together, no one will see the inside!

## I-CORDS

You will need double-pointed needles (DPN) to make the birds' legs and it is worth taking the time to master the very easy i-cord technique (see page 12), as the legs will be quicker to make and look neater. Alternatively, work the legs in stocking (stockinette) stitch and sew up the seam. If you have not used this technique before, please see page 12 for instructions.

## MAKING UP

Instructions for making up the birds are at the end of each pattern. It is worth taking your time when sewing the birds together. Finishing your birds carefully and neatly helps to make their little personalities shine. I like to view the making up of the birds as separate from the knitting.

If you are unsure about where to place the eyes, here are some tips. Sew the head up and stuff with toy filling. Push the eyes through the knitting. If you are not sure they are in the right place, go away, have a cup of tea (and a biscuit) – then go back to have another look. It will be obvious if they are not right and you can then adjust their position (see page 21 for detailed instructions on how to fit the eyes). You will also find the project photographs useful at this stage.

## ABBREVIATIONS

| | | | |
|---|---|---|---|
| **CDD** | centre double decrease; slip the next 2 stitches, as if knitting them together, K1, pass slipped stitches over, making a central decrease | **P2tog** | purl 2 stitches together |
| | | **P2togtbl** | purl 2 stitches together, through the back of the loops |
| **DPN** | double-pointed needle(s) | **psso** | pass slipped stitch over |
| **in** | inch(es) | **RS** | right side(s) |
| **K** | knit | **sl1** | slip 1 stitch |
| **Kfb** | knit into the front and back of the stitch, making 1 extra stitch | **ssK** | slip 2 sts knitwise one at a time, knit both stitches together through the back of the loops |
| **K2tog** | knit 2 stitches together | **SS** | stocking stitch (US stockinette stitch) |
| **m** | metre(s) | **st(s)** | stitch(es) |
| **mm** | millimetre(s) | **w&t** | wrap and turn (see Techniques, page 16) |
| **M1** | make 1 stitch (see Techniques, page 18) | **WS** | wrong side(s) |
| **P** | purl | **yd** | yard(s) |
| **Pfb** | purl into the front and back of the stitch, making 1 extra stitch | **yo** | yarn over |

# THE PROJECTS

# BLACKBIRD

## Instructions

### BODY AND HEAD

Using black yarn, cast on 14 sts and purl 1 row.

Work increase rows as follows (the first row is written out in full to enable you to see the pattern of the increases):

**Next row (RS):** K1, Kfb, K1, Kfb, Kfb, K1, Kfb, Kfb, K1, Kfb, Kfb, K1, Kfb, K1 (22 sts).

**Next row:** purl.

**Next row:** K1, (Kfb, K3, Kfb) to last st, K1 (30 sts).

**Next row:** purl.

**Next row:** K1, (Kfb, K5, Kfb) to last st, K1 (38 sts).

**Next row:** purl.

**Next row:** K1, (Kfb, K7, Kfb) to last st, K1 (46 sts).

Starting with a purl row, work 9 rows in SS.

**Next row:** K4, w&t.

**Next row:** purl to the end of the row.

**Next row:** knit.

**Next row:** P4, w&t.

**Next row:** knit to the end of the row.

**Next row:** purl.

Continuing in SS, cast off 10 sts at beginning of next 2 rows (26 sts).

**Next row:** K1, ssK, K to last 3 sts, K2tog, K1 (24 sts).

**Next row:** P1, P2tog, P to last 3 sts, P2togtbl, P1 (22 sts).

**Next row:** K1, (ssK, K1, K2tog). four times, K1 (14 sts).

Starting with a purl row, work 3 rows in SS.

**Next row:** K1, (ssK, K2tog) three times, K1 (8 sts).

Thread yarn through remaining sts, leaving a length of yarn for sewing up.

### WING (MAKE TWO)

Using black yarn, cast on 5 sts and work as follows:

**Next row:** (P1, K1) twice, P1.

**Next row:** Kfb, P1, K1, Pfb, K1 (7 sts).

**Next row:** (P1, K2) twice, P1.

**Next row:** (K1, Pfb, P1) twice, Kfb (10 sts).

**Next row:** Kfb, (P1, K1) four times, Pfb (12 sts).

**Next row:** (P1, K1) six times. Repeat last row five more times.

**Next row:** cast off 2 sts, (K1, P1) four times, K1 (10 sts).

**Next row:** (P1, K1) five times.

**Next row:** cast off 2 sts, (K1, P1) twice, K1, P2tog (7 sts).

**Next row:** (K1, P1) three times, K1.

**Next row:** cast off 2 sts, K1, P1, K2tog (4 sts).

**Next row:** (P1, K1) twice.

**Next row:** cast off 2 sts, K1 (2 sts).

**Next row:** P1, K1.

**Next row:** P2tog, threading yarn through remaining st to fasten.

### TAIL

Using black yarn, cast on 7 sts and work as follows:

**Next row:** (P1, K2) twice, P1.

**Next row:** (K1, P2) twice, K1. Repeat last 2 rows twice more (6 rows in total).

**Next row:** (P1, K2) twice, P1.

**Next row:** (K1, P2tog) twice, K1 (5 sts).

**Next row:** (P1, K1) twice, P1.

**Next row:** P2tog, K1, P2tog (3 sts). Cast off.

## MATERIALS

→ **DK (light worsted/8-ply) yarn:**
  30m (33yd) in black
  10m (11yd) in yellow
→ Two 5mm (¼in) black safety eyes
→ 2cm (¾in) square of yellow felt
→ Toy filling

## NEEDLES AND NOTIONS

→ 3mm (US 2 or 3, UK 11) knitting needles and DPN
→ Darning needle
→ Sharp scissors
→ Pins

## TENSION

→ 7 sts measured over 2.5cm (1in) and worked in SS using 3mm (US 2 or 3, UK 11) needles

## FINISHED SIZE

→ 10cm (4in) from beak to tail

GARDEN BIRDS

GARDEN BIRDS

## FOOT AND LEG (MAKE TWO)

Using yellow yarn and DPN, cast on 4 sts and work as follows:

**Next row:** cast off 3 sts (1 st).

*__*Next row:__* cast on 3 sts (4 sts).

**Next row:** cast off 3 sts (1 st).*

Work from * to * once more to make three toes, leaving 1 st.

With RS facing pick up and knit 2 more stitches across the top of the toes (3 sts).

Work 5 rows in SS using the i-cord technique (see page 12).

Thread yarn through sts, leaving a length of yarn for sewing up.

## BEAK

Using yellow yarn and 3mm (US 2 or 3, UK 11) needles, cast on 4 sts and knit 1 row.

**Next row:** (P2tog) twice (2 sts).

Thread yarn through remaining sts, leaving a length of yarn for sewing up.

## MAKING UP

First, follow the instructions on page 20 for mounting the safety eyes onto the felt backing and refer to page 21 for general making up instructions.

Taking the body and starting at the cast-off edge (top of the head), sew the seam, stopping when you reach the cast-off stitches at the back of the head. Place some toy filling inside the head – this will enable you to see exactly how the eyes look before you secure them. Taking the beak, sew the side seam and pin in place, approximately level with the cast-off stitches along the back of the bird.

Thread the eyes through the knitting, using the photographs for guidance. Remove the toy filling and beak and push the backs onto the safety eyes to secure them. Re-stuff the head with toy filling. Replace the beak and sew firmly in place.

Continue sewing the seam along the back of the bird until you reach the cast-on edge, stuffing with toy filling as you go. Thread the yarn through the cast-on stitches, gather and secure.

Pin the tail in place so that the cast-off edge is approximately 2cm (¾in) from the back of the body. Sew firmly in place.

Taking the wings, pin them in place on either side of the back centre seam using the photographs for guidance. Sew each wing in place along the front edge and also approximately 2cm (¾in) along the top edge.

With the 'toes' at the front and using the photographs for guidance, pin the legs in place either side of the gathered cast-off edge. Sew firmly in place.

# ROBIN

## MATERIALS

→ **DK (light worsted/8-ply) yarn:**
   - 30m (33yd) in brown
   - 10m (11yd) in red
   - 10m (11yd) in cream
   - 10m (11yd) in black
→ Two 5mm (¼in) black safety eyes
→ Toy filling

## NEEDLES AND NOTIONS

→ 3mm (US 2 or 3, UK 11) knitting needles and DPN
→ Darning needle
→ Sharp scissors
→ Pins

## TENSION

→ 7 sts measured over 2.5cm (1in) and worked in SS using 3mm (US 2 or 3, UK 11) needles

## FINISHED SIZE

→ 11cm (4¼in) from beak to tail

## Instructions

### BODY AND HEAD

Using brown yarn, cast on 14 sts and purl 1 row.
Work increase rows as follows (the first row is written out in full to enable you to see the pattern of the increases):
**Next row (RS):** K1, Kfb, K1, Kfb, Kfb, K1, Kfb, Kfb, K1, Kfb, Kfb, K1, Kfb, K1 (22 sts).
Join in cream yarn and work as follows:

|  | BROWN | CREAM | BROWN |
|---|---|---|---|
| **NEXT ROW:** | P8, | P6, | P8. |
| **NEXT ROW:** | K1, Kfb, K3, (Kfb) twice, | K3, (Kfb) twice, K3, | (Kfb) twice, K3, Kfb, K1 (30 sts). |
| **NEXT ROW:** | P9, | P12, | P9. |
| **NEXT ROW:** | K1, Kfb, K5, (Kfb) twice, | K5, (Kfb) twice, K5, | (Kfb) twice, K5, Kfb, K1 (38 sts). |

Join in red yarn and work as follows, carrying the cream yarn across the back of the work:

|  | BROWN | CREAM | RED | CREAM | BROWN |
|---|---|---|---|---|---|
| **NEXT ROW:** | P11, | P4, | P8, | P4, | P11. |
| **NEXT ROW:** | K1, Kfb, K7, (Kfb) twice, | K3, | K4, (Kfb) twice, K4, | K3, | (Kfb) twice, K7, Kfb, K1 (46 sts). |
| **NEXT ROW:** | P13, | P3, | P14, | P3, | P13. |
| **NEXT ROW:** | K13, | K2, | K16, | K2, | K13. |
| **NEXT ROW:** | P13, | P1, | P18, | P1, | P13. |

31

Break off cream yarn and work as follows:

| | BROWN | RED | BROWN |
|---|---|---|---|
| **NEXT ROW:** | K13, | K20, | K13. |
| **NEXT ROW:** | P13, | P20, | P13. |
| **NEXT ROW:** | K13, | K20, | K13. |
| **NEXT ROW:** | P13, | P20, | P13. |
| **NEXT ROW:** | K14, | K18, | K14. |
| **NEXT ROW:** | P14, | P18, | P14. |
| **NEXT ROW:** | K4, w&t, purl back across these 4 sts. Turn work and K15, | K16, | K15. |
| **NEXT ROW:** | P4, w&t, purl back across these 4 sts. Turn work and P15, | P16, | P15. |
| **NEXT ROW:** | Cast off 10 sts, K5, | K14, | K16 (36 sts). |
| **NEXT ROW:** | Cast off 10 sts, P6, | P12, | P7 (26 sts). |
| **NEXT ROW:** | K1, ssK, K5, | K10, | K5, K2tog, K1 (24 sts). |
| **NEXT ROW:** | P1, P2tog, P5, | P8, | P5, P2togtbl, P1 (22 sts). |
| **NEXT ROW:** | K1, ssK, K1, K2tog, ssK, | K1, K2tog, ssK, K1, | K2tog, ssK, K1, K2tog, K1 (14 sts). |
| **NEXT ROW:** | P5, | P4, | P5. |
| **NEXT ROW:** | K6, | K2, | K6. |

Break off red yarn and continue using brown yarn only.
**Next row:** purl.
**Next row:** K1, (ssK, K2tog) three times, K1 (8 sts).
Thread yarn through remaining sts, leaving a length of yarn for sewing up.

## WING (MAKE TWO)

Using brown yarn, cast on 5 sts and work as follows:
**Next row:** (P1, K1) twice, P1.
**Next row:** Kfb, P1, K1, Pfb, K1 (7 sts).
**Next row:** (P1, K2) twice, P1.
**Next row:** (K1, Pfb, P1) twice, Kfb (10 sts).
**Next row:** Kfb, (P1, K1) four times, Pfb (12 sts).
**Next row:** (P1, K1) six times.
Repeat last row five more times.
**Next row:** cast off 2 sts, (K1, P1) four times, K1 (10 sts).
**Next row:** (P1, K1) five times.
**Next row:** cast off 2 sts, (K1, P1) twice, K1, P2tog (7 sts).
**Next row:** (K1, P1) three times, K1.
**Next row:** cast off 2 sts, K1, P1, K2tog (4 sts).

**Next row:** (P1, K1) twice.
**Next row:** cast off 2 sts, K1 (2 sts).
**Next row:** P1, K1.
**Next row:** P2tog, threading yarn through remaining st to fasten.

## TAIL

Using brown yarn, cast on 7 sts and work as follows:
**Next row:** (P1, K2) twice, P1.
**Next row:** (K1, P2) twice, K1.
Repeat last 2 rows twice more (6 rows in total).
**Next row:** (P1, K2) twice, P1.
**Next row:** (K1, P2tog) twice, K1 (5 sts).
**Next row:** (P1, K1) twice, P1.
**Next row:** P2tog, K1, P2tog (3 sts).
Cast off.

## FOOT AND LEG (MAKE TWO)

Using black yarn and DPN, cast on 4 sts and work as follows:
**Next row:** cast off 3 sts (1 st).
***Next row:** cast on 3 sts (4 sts).
**Next row:** cast off 3 sts (1 st).*
Work from * to * once more to make three toes, leaving 1 st.
With RS facing pick up and knit 2 more stitches across the top of the toes (3 sts).
Work 5 rows in SS using the i-cord technique (see page 12).
Thread yarn through sts, leaving a length of yarn for sewing up.

## BEAK

Using black yarn and 3mm (US 2 or 3, UK 11) needles, cast on 4 sts and knit 1 row.
**Next row:** P2tog twice (2 sts).
Thread yarn through remaining sts, leaving a length of yarn for sewing up.

## MAKING UP

Refer to page 21 for general making up instructions.

Taking the body and starting at the cast-off edge (top of the head), sew the seam, stopping when you reach the cast-off stitches at the back of the head. Place some toy filling inside the head – this will enable you to see exactly how the eyes look before you secure them. Taking the beak, sew the side seam and pin in place, approximately level with the cast-off stitches along the back of the bird.

Thread the eyes through the knitting, using the photographs for guidance. Remove the toy filling and beak and push the backs onto the safety eyes to secure them. Re-stuff the head with toy filling. Replace the beak and sew firmly in place.

Continue sewing the seam along the back of the bird until you reach the cast-on edge, stuffing with toy filling as you go. Thread the yarn through the cast-on stitches, gather and secure.

Pin the tail in place so the cast-off edge is approximately 2cm (¾in) from the back of the body. Sew firmly in place.

Taking the wings, pin them in place on either side of the back centre seam using the photographs for guidance. Sew each wing in place along the front edge and for approximately 2cm (¾in) along the top edge.

With the 'toes' at the front and using the photographs for guidance, pin the legs in place either side of the gathered cast-off edge. Sew firmly in place.

# BLUE TIT

## Instructions

### MATERIALS

→ **DK (light worsted/8-ply) yarn:**
  10m (11yd) in lime yellow
  10m (11yd) in green
  10m (11yd) in blue
  10m (11yd) in cream
  10m (11yd) in black
→ Two 5mm (¼in) black safety eyes
→ Toy filling

### NEEDLES AND NOTIONS

→ 3mm (US 2 or 3, UK 11)
  knitting needles and DPN
→ Darning needle
→ Sharp scissors
→ Pins

### TENSION

→ 7 sts measured over 2.5cm (1in)
  and worked in SS using 3mm
  (US 2 or 3, UK 11) needles

### FINISHED SIZE

→ 11cm (4¼in) from beak to tail

### BODY AND HEAD

Using yellow yarn, cast on 14 sts and purl 1 row.
Work increase rows as follows (the first row is written out in full to enable you to see the pattern of the increases):
**Next row (RS):** K1, Kfb, K1, Kfb, Kfb, K1, Kfb, Kfb, K1, Kfb, Kfb, K1, Kfb, K1 (22 sts).
**Next row:** purl.
**Next row:** K1, (Kfb, K3, Kfb) to last st, K1 (30 sts).
**Next row:** purl.
**Next row:** K1, (Kfb, K5, Kfb) to last st, K1 (38 sts).
**Next row:** purl.
**Next row:** K1, (Kfb, K7, Kfb) to last st, K1 (46 sts).
**Next row:** purl.

| | GREEN | YELLOW | GREEN |
|---|---|---|---|
| **NEXT ROW:** | K7, | K32, | K7. |
| **NEXT ROW:** | P8, | P30, | P8. |
| **NEXT ROW:** | K10, | K26, | K10. |
| **NEXT ROW:** | P12, | P22, | P12. |
| **NEXT ROW:** | K14, | K18, | K14. |
| **NEXT ROW:** | P15, | P16, | P15. |
| **NEXT ROW:** | K16, | K14, | K16. |
| **NEXT ROW:** | P16, | P14, | P16. |
| **NEXT ROW:** | K4, w&t, purl back across these 4 sts. Turn work, cast off 11 sts, K7, | K8, | K19 (35 sts). |
| **NEXT ROW:** | P4, w&t, knit back across these 4 sts. Turn work, cast off 11 sts, | CHANGE TO BLACK YARN and purl to the end of the row (24 sts). | |

**Next row:** using black yarn, knit 1 row.
Join in cream yarn and work as follows:

| | CREAM | BLACK | CREAM |
|---|---|---|---|
| **NEXT ROW:** | P10, | P4, | P10. |
| **NEXT ROW:** | K11, | K2, | K11. |
| **NEXT ROW:** | P11, | P2, | P11. |

Using black yarn, knit 1 row. Break off black yarn.
Using cream yarn and starting with a purl row, work 2 rows in SS. Break off cream yarn, join in blue yarn and work as follows:
**Next row:** P1, (P2tog, P3, P2togtbl) three times, P2 (18 sts).
**Next row:** knit.
**Next row:** (P2tog) nine times (9 sts).
Thread yarn through remaining sts, leaving a length of yarn for sewing up.

## WING (MAKE TWO)

Using blue yarn, cast on 5 sts and work as follows:
**Next row:** (P1, K1) twice, P1.
**Next row:** Kfb, P1, K1, Pfb, K1 (7 sts).
**Next row:** (P1, K2) twice, P1.
**Next row:** (K1, Pfb, P1) twice, Kfb (10 sts).
**Next row:** Kfb, (P1, K1) four times, Pfb (12 sts).
**Next row:** (P1, K1) six times. Repeat last row once more.
Without breaking off the blue yarn, join in cream yarn and work as follows:
**Next row:** (P1, K1) six times. Repeat last row once more.

Break off cream yarn, change to blue yarn and work as follows:
**Next row:** (P1, K1) six times. Repeat last row once more.
**Next row:** cast off 2 sts, (K1, P1) four times, K1 (10 sts).
**Next row:** (P1, K1) five times.
**Next row:** cast off 2 sts, (K1, P1) twice, K1, P2tog (7 sts).
**Next row:** (K1, P1) three times, K1.
**Next row:** cast off 2 sts, K1, P1, K2tog (4 sts).
**Next row:** (P1, K1) twice.
**Next row:** cast off 2 sts, K1 (2 sts).
**Next row:** P1, K1.
**Next row:** P2tog, threading yarn through remaining st to fasten.

## TAIL

Using blue yarn, cast on 7 sts and work as follows:

**Next row:** (P1, K2) twice, P1.
**Next row:** (K1, P2) twice, K1.
Repeat last 2 rows twice more (6 rows in total).
**Next row:** (P1, K2) twice, P1.
**Next row:** (K1, P2tog) twice, K1 (5 sts).
**Next row:** (P1, K1) twice, P1.
**Next row:** P2tog, K1, P2tog (3 sts).
Cast off.

## FOOT AND LEG (MAKE TWO)

Using black yarn and DPN, cast on 4 sts and work as follows:
**Next row:** cast off 3 sts (1 st).
*****Next row:** cast on 3 sts (4 sts).
**Next row:** cast off 3 sts (1 st).*****

Work from * to * once more to make three toes, leaving 1 st. With RS facing pick up and knit 2 more stitches across the top of the toes (3 sts).
Work 5 rows in SS using the i-cord technique (see page 12).
Thread yarn through sts, leaving a length of yarn for sewing up.

## BEAK

Using black yarn and DPN, cast on 4 sts and knit 1 row.
**Next row:** (P2tog) twice (2 sts).
Thread yarn through remaining sts, leaving a length of yarn for sewing up.

## MAKING UP

Refer to page 21 for general making up instructions.

Taking the body and starting at the cast-off edge (top of the head), sew the seam, stopping when you reach the cast-off stitches at the back of the head. Place some toy filling inside the head – this will enable you to see exactly how the eyes look before you secure them. Taking the beak, sew the side seam and pin in place, approximately level with the cast-off stitches along the back of the bird.

Thread the eyes through the knitting, using the photographs for guidance. Remove the toy filling and beak and push the backs onto the safety eyes to secure them. Re-stuff the head with toy filling. Replace the beak and sew firmly in place.

Continue sewing the seam along the back of the bird until you reach the cast-on edge, stuffing with toy filling as you go. Thread the yarn through the cast-on stitches, gather and secure.

Pin the tail in place so that the cast-off edge is approximately 2cm (¾in) from the back of the body. Sew firmly in place.

Pin the wings in place on either side of the back centre seam using the photographs for guidance. Sew each wing in place along the front edge and for approximately 2cm (¾in) along the top edge.

With the 'toes' at the front and using the photographs for guidance, pin the legs in place either side of the gathered cast-off edge. Sew firmly in place.

# WOODPECKER

## Instructions

### BODY AND HEAD

Using pale green yarn, cast on 14 sts and purl 1 row.
Work increase rows as follows (the first row is written out in full to enable you to see the pattern of the increases):
**Next row:** K1, Kfb, K1, Kfb, Kfb, K1, Kfb, Kfb, K1, Kfb, Kfb, K1, Kfb, K1 (22 sts).
**Next row:** purl.
**Next row:** K1, (Kfb, K3, Kfb) to last st, K1 (30 sts).
**Next row:** purl.
**Next row:** K1, (Kfb, K5, Kfb) to last st, K1 (38 sts).
**Next row:** purl.
**Next row:** K1, M1, K17, M1, K2, M1, K17, M1, K1 (42 sts).
Starting with a purl row, work 3 rows in SS.
**Next row:** K39, w&t.
**Next row:** P36, w&t.
**Next row:** knit to the end of the row.
**Next row:** purl.
Continuing in SS, cast off 3 sts at the beginning of the next 2 rows (36 sts).
**Next row:** K1, ssK, K to last 3 sts, K2tog, K1 (34 sts).
**Next row:** purl.
**Next row:** K1, ssK, K11, K2tog, K2, ssK, K11, K2tog, K1 (30 sts).
**Next row:** purl.
**Next row:** K1, ssK, K9, K2tog, K2, ssK, K9, K2tog, K1 (26 sts).
**Next row:** purl.
**Next row:** K1, ssK, K7, K2tog, K2, ssK, K7, K2tog, K1 (22 sts).
**Next row:** purl.
**Next row:** K1, ssK, K5, K2tog, K2, ssK, K5, K2tog, K1 (18 sts).
**Next row:** P1, P2tog, P3, P2togtbl, P2, P2tog, P3, P2togtbl, P1 (14 sts).
**Next row:** knit.
**Next row:** P1, M1, P5, M1, P2, M1, P5, M1, P1 (18 sts).
**Next row:** K1, M1, K7, M1, K2, M1, K7, M1, K1 (22 sts).
**Next row:** P1, M1, P9, M1, P2, M1, P9, M1, P1 (26 sts).
Starting with a knit row, work 4 rows in SS.
Change to red yarn and, starting with a knit row, work 2 rows in SS.
**Next row:** K1, ssK, K7, K2tog, K2, ssK, K7, K2tog, K1 (22 sts).
**Next row:** P1, P2tog, P5, P2togtbl, P2, P2tog, P5, P2togtbl, P1 (18 sts).
**Next row:** K1, ssK, K3, K2tog, K2, ssK, K3, K2tog, K1 (14 sts).

## MATERIALS

→ **DK (light worsted/8-ply) yarn:**
   30m (33yd) in pale green
   20m (22yd) in dark green
   10m (11yd) in black
   10m (11yd) in red
   10m (11yd) in gold
   10m (11yd) in grey
→ Two 5mm (¼in) black safety eyes
→ 2cm (¾in) square of white felt
→ Toy filling

## NEEDLES AND NOTIONS

→ 3mm (US 2 or 3, UK 11) knitting needles and DPN
→ Darning needle
→ Sharp scissors
→ Pins
→ Spare needle or stitch holder

## TENSION

→ 7 sts measured over 2.5cm (1in) and worked in SS using 3mm (US 2 or 3, UK 11) needles

## FINISHED SIZE

→ 11cm (4¼in) from top of head to feet

Divide the remaining sts in half, so that 7 sts are on one needle and 7 sts are on another. With RS together, fold the work in half and cast off using the three-needle cast-off technique (see page 15).

## WING: MAKE TWO

Using dark green yarn, cast on 5 sts and work as follows:
**Next row:** (P1, K1) twice, P1.
**Next row:** Kfb, P1, K1, Pfb, K1 (7 sts).
**Next row:** (P1, K2) twice, P1.
**Next row:** (K1, Pfb, P1) twice, Kfb (10 sts).
**Next row:** Kfb, (P1, K1) four times, Pfb (12 sts).
**Next row:** (P1, K1) six times.
Repeat last row five more times.
**Next row:** K2tog, (P1, K1) five times (11 sts).
**Next row:** (P1, K1) four times, P1, K2tog (10 sts).
**Next row:** K2tog, (P1, K1) four times (9 sts).
**Next row:** (P1, K1) three times, P1, K2tog. (8 sts).
**Next row:** K2tog, (P1, K1) three times (7 sts).
**Next row:** (P1, K1) twice, P1, K2tog (6 sts).
**Next row:** K2tog, (P1, K1) twice (5 sts).
**Next row:** P1, K1, P1, K2tog (4 sts).
**Next row:** K2tog, P1, K1 (3 sts).
**Next row:** P1, K2tog (2 sts).
**Next row:** K2tog, threading yarn through remaining st to fasten.

## WING EDGING (MAKE TWO)

Using black yarn, cast on 3 sts and, starting with a knit row, work 2 rows in SS.
*Change to gold yarn.
Starting with a knit row, work 2 rows in SS.
Change to black yarn.
Starting with a knit row, work 2 rows in SS.*
Work from * to * five more times.
Cast off using black yarn.

## FACE SECTION (RIGHT SIDE)

Using red yarn, cast on 7 sts.
**Next row:** cast off 3 sts knitwise, change to black yarn and knit to the end of the row (4 sts).
**Next row:** purl.
**Next row:** cast on 1 st, K4, w&t (wrap last st).
**Next row:** purl to the end of the row (5 sts).
**Next row:** cast on 1 st, K5, w&t (wrap last st).
Purl to the end of the row (6 sts).
Cast off.

## FACE SECTION (LEFT SIDE)

Using red yarn, cast on 7 sts.
**Next row:** cast off 3 sts purlwise, change to black yarn and purl to the end of the row (4 sts).
**Next row:** knit.
**Next row:** cast on 1 st, P4, w&t (wrap last st).
**Next row:** knit to the end of the row (5 sts).
**Next row:** cast on 1 st, P5, w&t (wrap last st).
Knit to the end of the row (6 sts).
Cast off.

## TAIL

Using dark green yarn, cast on 7 sts and work as follows:

**Next row:** K3, sl1, K3.
**Next row:** purl.
Repeat last 2 rows twice more.
**Next row:** K1, M1, K2, sl1, K2, M1, K1 (9 sts).
**Next row:** purl.
**Next row:** K4, sl1, K4.
**Next row:** purl.
**Next row:** K3, K2tog, turn work.
**Next row:** P2tog, P2.
**Next row:** K1, K2tog, turn work.
**Next row:** P2tog.
Thread yarn through remaining sts to fasten.
With RS facing, rejoin yarn to remaining 4 sts and knit 1 row.
**Next row:** P2, P2togtbl.
**Next row:** ssK, K1.
**Next row:** P2tog.
Thread yarn through remaining sts to fasten.

## FOOT (MAKE TWO)

Using grey yarn and DPN, cast on 6 sts.
 **Next row:** cast off 4 sts, K1 (2 sts).
*Next row: K2.
 **Next row:** cast on 4 sts, cast off 4 sts, K1 (2 sts)*.
Work from * to * once more to make a third toe, casting off 5 sts on last row (1 st).
With RS facing, pick up and knit 2 sts across the top of the toes (3 sts).
Work 3 rows in SS using the i-cord technique (see page 12).
Thread yarn through sts, leaving a length of yarn for sewing up.

## BEAK

Using grey yarn and 3mm (US 2 or 3, UK 11) needles, cast on 5 sts and work as follows:

**Next row:** K2, sl1, K2.
**Next row:** purl.
Repeat last 2 rows once more.
**Next row:** K1, CDD, K1 (3 sts).
**Next row:** purl.
**Next row:** CDD (1 st).
Thread yarn through remaining st, leaving a length of yarn for sewing up.

## MAKING UP

First, follow the instructions on page 20 for mounting the safety eyes onto the felt backing and refer to page 21 for general making up instructions.

Taking the body and starting at the cast-off edge (top of the head), sew the seam along the shaped edge, stopping when you reach the cast-off stitches at the back of the head.

Place some toy filling inside the head. Taking the two face pieces, sew them together in the middle with the red section at the bottom.

Pin the face pieces for your bird in place, using the photographs for guidance, and then sew to the head.

Taking the beak, sew the side seam and pin in place, approximately level with the cast-off stitches along the back of the bird. Use the photographs for guidance.

Thread the safety eyes through the knitting. When you are happy with their position, remove the toy filling and beak and push the backs onto the safety eyes to secure them. Re-stuff the head with toy filling. Replace the beak and sew firmly in place.

Continue sewing the seam along the back of the bird until you reach the cast-on edge, stuffing the body with toy filling as you go. Thread the yarn through the cast-on stitches, gather and secure.

Taking a wing and a wing edging, carefully sew the edging along the sloped edge of the wing. Repeat for the second wing.

Taking the wings, pin them in place on either side of the back centre seam using the photograph for guidance. Sew each wing in place around the top edges.

Taking the tail, sew the cast-on edge in place on the back of the woodpecker, just above the start of the decreases for the back.

With the 'toes' at the front and, using the photographs for guidance, pin the feet in place, either side of the gathered cast-off edge. Sew firmly in position.

# KINGFISHER

## MATERIALS

→ **DK (light worsted/8-ply) yarn:**
  20m (22yd) in orange
  30m (33yd) in turquoise
  10m (11yd) in grey
  10m (11yd) in cream
  1m (1yd) in black
→ Two 5mm (¼in) black safety eyes
→ 2cm (¾in) square of orange felt
→ Toy filling

## NEEDLES AND NOTIONS

→ 3mm (US 2 or 3, UK 11) knitting needles and DPN
→ Darning needle
→ Sharp scissors
→ Pins
→ Spare needle or stitch holder

## TENSION

→ 7 sts measured over 2.5cm (1in) and worked in SS using 3mm (US 2 or 3, UK 11) needles

## FINISHED SIZE

→ 12cm (4¾in) tall from head to base

## Instructions

### BODY AND HEAD

Using orange yarn, cast on 14 sts and purl 1 row.
Work increase rows as follows (the first row is written out in full to enable you to see the pattern of the increases):
**Next row:** K1, Kfb, K1, Kfb, Kfb, K1, Kfb, Kfb, K1, Kfb, Kfb, K1, Kfb, K1 (22 sts).
**Next row:** purl.
**Next row:** K1, (Kfb, K3, Kfb) to last st, K1 (30 sts).
**Next row:** purl.
**Next row:** K1, (Kfb, K5, Kfb) to last st, K1 (38 sts).
**Next row:** purl.
**Next row:** K1, M1, K17, M1, K2, M1, K17, M1, K1 (42 sts).
Get two skeins of turquoise yarn ready so that you can use one at the beginning of the row and one at the end of the row.

**COUNTRYSIDE BIRDS**

|  | TURQUOISE | ORANGE | TURQUOISE |
|---|---|---|---|
| NEXT ROW: | P3, | P36, | P3. |
| NEXT ROW: | K5, | K32, | K5. |
| NEXT ROW: | P7, | P28, | P7. |
| NEXT ROW: | K8, | K26, | K5, w&t. |
| NEXT ROW: | P6, | P24, | P6, w&t. |
| NEXT ROW: | K6, | K24, | K9. |
| NEXT ROW: | P10, | P22, | P10. |
| NEXT ROW: | cast off 3 sts, K7, | K20, | K11 (33 sts). |
| NEXT ROW: | cast off 3 sts, P8, | P18, | P9 (36 sts). |
| NEXT ROW: | K1, ssK, K7, | K16, | K7, K2tog, K1 (34 sts). |
| NEXT ROW: | P9, | P16, | P9. |
| NEXT ROW: | K1, ssK, K6, | K5, K2tog, K2, ssK, K5, | K6, K2tog, K1 (30 sts). |
| NEXT ROW: | P5, | P20, | P5. |

Break off orange yarn. Join in cream yarn and work as follows (I carried the cream yarn along the row on the reverse of the work, making sure not to pull the yarn too tightly and kept using two separate strands of turquoise yarn):

|  | CREAM | TURQUOISE | CREAM | TURQUOISE | CREAM |
|---|---|---|---|---|---|
| NEXT ROW: | K1, ssK, K2, | K5, | K2, K2tog, K2, ssK, K2, | K5, | K2, K2tog, K2 (26 sts). |
| NEXT ROW: | P4, | P5, | P8, | P5, | P4. |
| NEXT ROW: | K1, ssK, K2, | K5, | K2tog, K2, ssK, | K5, | K2, K2tog, K1 (22 sts). |
| NEXT ROW: | P1, P2tog, P1, | P4, P2togtbl, | P2, | P2tog, P4, | P1, P2togtbl, P1 (18 sts). |

Break off cream yarn and continue using turquoise yarn only.
**Next row:** K1, M1, K7, M1, K2, M1, K7, M1, K1 (22 sts).
**Next row:** P1, M1, P9, M1, P2, M1, P9, M1, P1 (26 sts).
Starting with a knit row, work 6 rows in SS.
**Next row:** K1, ssK, K7, K2tog, K2, ssK, K7, K2tog, K1 (22 sts).

**Next row:** P1, P2tog, P5, P2togtbl, P2, P2tog, P5, P2togtbl, P1 (18 sts).
**Next row:** K6, K2tog, K2, ssK, K6 (16 sts).
Divide the remaining sts in half, so that 8 sts are on one needle and 8 sts are on another. With RS together, fold work in half and cast off using the three-needle cast-off technique (see page 15).

## WING (MAKE TWO)

Using turquoise yarn cast on 7 sts and work as follows:
**Next row:** Kfb, (P1, K1) twice, P1, Kfb (9 sts).
**Next row:** (K1, P1) four times, K1.
**Next row:** Kfb, (K1, P1) three times, K1, Pfb (11 sts).
**Next row:** Kfb, (K1, P1) four times, K1, Pfb (13 sts).
**Next row:** (P1, K1) six times, P1.
**Next row:** Pfb, (P1, K1) five times, P1, Kfb (15 sts).
**Next row:** (K1, P1) seven times, K1.
**Next row:** (P1, K1) seven times, P1.
Repeat last 2 rows twice more.
**Next row:** K2tog, (K1, P1) six times, K1 (14 sts).
**Next row:** (P1, K1) six times, K2tog (13 sts).
**Next row:** K2tog, (K1, P1) five times, K1 (12 sts).
**Next row:** (P1, K1) five times, K2tog (11 sts).
**Next row:** K2tog, (K1, P1) four times, K1 (10 sts).
**Next row:** (P1, K1) four times, K2tog (9 sts).
**Next row:** K2tog, (K1,P1) three times, K1 (8 sts).
**Next row:** (P1, K1) three times, K2tog (7 sts).
**Next row:** K2tog, (K1, P1) twice, K1 (6 sts).
**Next row:** (P1, K1) twice, K2tog (5 sts).
**Next row:** K2tog, K1, P1, K1 (4 sts).
**Next row:** P1, K1, K2tog (3 sts).
**Next row:** K2tog, K1 (2 sts).
**Next row:** K2tog, threading yarn through remaining st to fasten.

## FACE SECTION (RIGHT SIDE)

Using orange yarn, cast on 5 sts and purl 1 row.
**Next row:** K3, w&t.
**Next row:** purl to end of row.
Cast off all sts knitwise.

## FACE SECTION (LEFT SIDE)

Using orange yarn cast on 5 sts and knit 1 row.
**Next row:** P3, w&t.
**Next row:** knit to the end of the row.
Cast off all sts purlwise.

## TAIL

Using turquoise yarn, cast on 10 sts.
Starting with a knit row, work 4 rows in SS.
**Next row:** K1, ssK, K to last 3 sts, K2tog, K1. (8 sts).
**Next row:** purl.
Repeat last 2 rows twice more (4 sts).
**Next row:** K1, K2tog, K1 (3 sts).
Knit 1 row to form a fold line.
Change to orange yarn and starting with a knit row, work 4 rows in SS.

**Next row:** (K1, M1) twice, K1 (5 sts).
**Next row:** purl.
**Next row:** K1, M1, K3, M1, K1 (7 sts).
**Next row:** purl.
Cast off.

## FOOT (MAKE TWO)

Using grey yarn and DPN cast on 6 sts.
**Next row:** cast off 4 sts, K1 (2 sts).
**\*Next row:** K2.
**Next row:** cast on 4 sts, cast off 4 sts, K1 (2 sts)\*.
Work from \* to \* once more to make a third toe, casting off 5 sts on the last row (1 st).
With RS facing, pick up and knit 2 sts across the top of the toes (3 sts).
Work 3 rows in SS using the i-cord technique (see page 12).
Thread yarn through sts, leaving a length of yarn for sewing up.

## BEAK

Using black yarn and 3mm (US 2 or 3, UK 11) needles, cast on 5 sts and work as follows:
**Next row:** K2, sl1, K2.
**Next row:** purl.
Repeat last 2 rows twice more.
**Next row:** K1, CDD, K1 (3 sts).
**Next row:** purl.
**Next row:** CDD (1 st).
Thread yarn through remaining st, leaving a length of yarn for sewing up.

## MAKING UP

First, follow the instructions on page 20 for mounting the safety eyes onto the felt backing and refer to page 21 for general making up instructions.

Taking the body and starting at the cast-off edge (top of the head), sew the seam along the shaped edge, stopping when you reach the cast-off stitches at the back of the head.

Place some toy filling inside the head. Pin the face pieces for your bird in place, using the photographs for guidance and then sew to the head.

Taking the beak, sew the side seam and pin in place, approximately level with the cast-off stitches along the back of the bird. Use the photographs for guidance.

Thread the safety eyes through the knitting. When you are happy with their position, remove the toy filling and beak and push the backs onto the safety eyes to secure them. Re-stuff the head with toy filling. Replace the beak and sew firmly in place.

Continue sewing the seam along the back of the bird until you reach the cast-on edge, stuffing the body with toy filling as you go. Thread the yarn through the cast-on stitches, gather and secure.

Taking the wings, pin them in place on either side of the back centre seam using the photograph for guidance. Sew each wing in place around the top edges.

Taking the tail piece, fold in half at the fold line and sew the side seams. Place a small amount of toy filling inside the tail. Sew to the body by sewing the orange part of the tail to the orange lower body and the turquoise section to the turquoise top section of the body. Use the photographs for guidance.

With the 'toes' at the front and using the photographs for guidance, pin the feet in place, either side of the gathered cast-off edge. Sew firmly in place.

# PHEASANT

## MATERIALS

→ **DK (light worsted/8-ply) yarn:**
  20m (22yd) in rust brown
  20m (22yd) in red brown
  10m (11yd) in gold
  10m (11yd) in teal
  1m (1yd) in cream
  10m (11yd) in grey
  10m (11yd) in red
→ Two 5mm (¼in) black safety eyes
→ 2cm (¾in) square of yellow felt
→ Toy filling

## NEEDLES AND NOTIONS

→ 3mm (US 2 or 3, UK 11) knitting needles
  and DPN
→ Darning needle
→ Sharp scissors
→ Pins
→ Spare needle or stitch holders

## TENSION

→ 7 sts measured over 2.5cm (1in) and worked in
  SS using 3mm (US 2 or 3, UK 11) needles

## FINISHED SIZE

→ 11cm (4¼in) from top of head to feet

## Instructions

### BODY AND HEAD

Using rust brown yarn, cast on 14 sts and purl 1 row.
Work increase rows as follows (the first row is written out in
full to enable you to see the pattern of the increases):
**Next row:** K1, Kfb, K1, Kfb, Kfb, K1, Kfb, Kfb, K1, Kfb, Kfb, K1,
Kfb, K1.(22 sts).
**Next row:** purl.
**Next row:** K1, (Kfb, K3, Kfb) to last st, K1 (30 sts).

Get two skeins of red brown yarn ready so that you can use one at the beginning of the row and one at the end of the row and work as follows:

| NEXT ROW: | RED BROWN | RUST BROWN | RED BROWN |
|---|---|---|---|
| NEXT ROW: | P4, | P22, | P4. |
| NEXT ROW: | K1, Kfb, K3, | K2, (Kfb) twice, (K5, Kfb, Kfb) twice, K2, | K3, Kfb, K1 (38 sts). |
| NEXT ROW: | P7, | P24, | P7. |
| NEXT ROW: | K1, Kfb, K6, | K1, (Kfb) twice, (K7, Kfb, Kfb) twice, K1, | K6, Kfb, K1 (46 sts). |
| NEXT ROW: | P9, | P28, | P9. |
| NEXT ROW: | K10, | K26, | K10. |
| NEXT ROW: | P10, | P26, | P10. |
| NEXT ROW: | K11, | K24, | K8, w&t. |
| NEXT ROW: | P8, | P24, | P8, w&t. |
| NEXT ROW: | K9, | K22, | K12. |
| NEXT ROW: | P13, | P20, | P13. |
| NEXT ROW: | cast off 3 sts, K10, | K18, | K14 (43 sts). |
| NEXT ROW: | cast off 3 sts, P11, | P16, | P12 (40 sts). |
| NEXT ROW: | K1, ssK, K10, | K4, K2tog, K2, ssK, K4, | K10, K2tog, K1 (36 sts). |
| NEXT ROW: | P13, | P10, | P13. |
| NEXT ROW: | K1, ssK, K11, | K1, K2tog, K2, ssK, K1, | K11, K2tog, K1 (32 sts). |
| NEXT ROW: | P13, | P6, | P13. |
| NEXT ROW: | K1, ssK, K10, | K2tog, K2, ssK, | K10, K2tog, K1 (28 sts). |

Break off rust brown yarn and using red brown yarn work as follows:
**Next row:** purl.
**Next row:** K1, ssK, K8, K2tog, K2, ssK, K8, K2tog, K1 (24 sts).
**Next row:** P1, P2tog, P6, P2togtbl, P2, P2tog, P6, P2togtbl, P1 (20 sts).
**Next row:** K1, ssK, K4, K2tog, K2, ssK, K4, K2tog, K1 (16 sts).
**Next row:** purl.

Join in cream yarn and work as follows:

| NEXT ROW: | CREAM | RED BROWN | CREAM |
|---|---|---|---|
|  | K7, | K2, | K7. |

Break off red brown yarn and using cream yarn only, purl across all sts (16 sts).
Change to teal yarn.
Starting with a knit row, work 2 rows in SS.
**Next row:** K1, M1, K6, M1, K2, M1, K6, M1, K1 (20 sts).
**Next row:** P1, M1, P8, M1, P2, M1, P8, M1, P1 (24 sts).
Starting with a knit row, work 4 rows in SS.
**Next row:** K1, ssK, K6, K2tog, K2, ssK, K6, K2tog, K1 (20 sts).
**Next row:** P1, P2tog, P4, P2togtbl, P2, P2tog, P4, P2togtbl, P1 (16 sts).
**Next row:** K1, M1, K4, K2tog, K2, ssK, K4, M1, K1 (16 sts).
**Next row:** P1, M1, P14, M1, P1 (18 sts).
Divide the remaining sts in half so that 9 sts are on one needle and 9 sts are on another. With RS together, fold work in half and cast off using the three-needle cast-off technique (see page 15).

## WING (MAKE TWO)

Using red brown yarn, cast on 7 sts and work as follows:
**Next row:** Kfb, (P1, K1) twice, P1, Kfb (9 sts).
**Next row:** (K1, P1) four times, K1.
**Next row:** Kfb, (K1, P1) three times, K1, Pfb (11 sts).
**Next row:** Kfb, (K1, P1) four times, K1, Pfb (13 sts).
**Next row:** (P1, K1) six times, P1.
**Next row:** Pfb, (P1, K1) five times, P1, Kfb (15 sts).
**Next row:** (K1, P1) seven times, K1.
**Next row:** (P1, K1) seven times, P1.
Repeat last 2 rows twice more.
**Next row:** K2tog, (K1, P1) six times, K1 (14 sts).
**Next row:** (P1, K1) six times, K2tog (13 sts).
**Next row:** K2tog, (K1, P1) five times, K1 (12 sts).
**Next row:** (P1, K1) five times, K2tog (11 sts).
**Next row:** K2tog, (K1, P1) four times, K1 (10 sts).
**Next row:** (P1, K1) four times, K2tog (9 sts).
**Next row:** K2tog, (K1,P1) three times, K1 (8 sts).
**Next row:** (P1, K1) three times, K2tog (7 sts).
**Next row:** K2tog, (K1, P1) twice, K1 (6 sts).
**Next row:** (P1, K1) twice, K2tog (5 sts).
**Next row:** K2tog, K1, P1, K1 (4 sts).
**Next row:** P1, K1, K2tog (3 sts).

**Next row:** K2tog, K1 (2 sts).
**Next row:** K2tog, threading yarn through the remaining st to fasten.

## FACE SECTION

*Using red yarn, cast on 3 sts and work as follows:
**Next row:** (P1, M1) twice, P1 (5 sts).
**Next row:** K1, M1, K3, M1, K1 (7 sts).
**Next row:** P1, M1, P5, M1, P1 (9 sts)*.
Break off yarn, leaving sts on a spare needle or stitch holder.
Make a second section, working from * to * once more.
With RS facing, place both sections onto one needle and work across all sts as follows:
**Next row:** K1, M1, K7, K2tog, K7, M1, K1 (19 sts).
**Next row:** P7, P2tog, P1, P2togtbl, P7 (17 sts).
**Next row:** K7, w&t.
**Next row:** P4, w&t.
**Next row:** K11, w&t.
**Next row:** P4, w&t.
**Next row:** knit to the end of the row (17 sts).
Cast off all sts purlwise.

## TAIL FEATHER (MAKE THREE)

Note: Use either red brown or rust brown yarn for the contrast stripes, or mix it up and work one feather in one contrast colour and two feathers in the other contrast colour.
Using gold yarn, cast on 5 sts and work as follows:
*Next row: K2, sl1, K2.
**Next row:** purl.
Repeat last 2 rows once more.
Without breaking off gold yarn, join in contrast colour yarn.
**Next row:** K2, sl1, K2.
**Next row:** purl.
Change to gold yarn.*
Work from * to * twice more.
**Next row:** K2, sl1, K2.
**Next row:** purl.
**Next row:** K1, CDD, K1 (3 sts).
**Next row:** purl.
**Next row:** CDD (1 st).
Thread yarn through remaining st to fasten.

## FOOT (MAKE TWO)

Using grey yarn and DPN cast on 6 sts.
**Next row:** cast off 4 sts, K1 (2 sts).
**\*Next row:** K2.
**Next row:** cast on 4 sts, cast off 4 sts, K1.
(2 sts)\*.
Work from \* to \* once more to make a third toe,
casting off 5 sts on the last row (1 st).
With RS facing, pick up and knit 2 sts across the top
of the toes (3 sts).
Work 3 rows in SS using the i-cord technique (see
page 12).
Thread yarn through sts, leaving a length of yarn for
sewing up.

## BEAK

Using grey yarn and 3mm (US 2 or 3, UK 11)
knitting needles, cast on 5 sts and work as follows:
**Next row:** K2, sl1, K2.
**Next row:** purl.
Repeat last 2 rows once more.
**Next row:** K1, CDD, K1 (3 sts).
**Next row:** purl.
**Next row:** CDD (1 st).
Thread yarn through remaining st, leaving a length of
yarn for sewing up.

## MAKING UP

First, follow the instructions on page 20 for
mounting the safety eyes onto the felt backing and
refer to page 21 for general making up instructions.

Taking the body and starting at the cast-off edge
(top of the head), sew the seam along the shaped
edge, stopping when you reach the cast-off stitches
at the back of the head. Place some toy filling inside
the head. Pin the face section for your bird in place,
using the photographs for guidance and then sew to
the head.

Taking the beak, sew the side seam and pin in
place, approximately level with the cast-off stitches
along the back of the bird. Use the photographs
for guidance.

Thread the safety eyes through the knitting. When
you are happy with their position, remove the toy
filling and beak and push the backs onto the safety
eyes to secure them. Re-stuff the head with toy
filling. Replace the beak and sew firmly in place.

Continue sewing the seam along the back of
the bird until you reach the cast-on edge, stuffing
the body with toy filling as you go. Thread the yarn
through the cast-on stitches, gather and secure.

Taking the wings, pin them in place on either side
of the back centre seam using the photograph
for guidance. Sew each wing in place around the
top edges.

Taking the three tail feathers, pin two in place
slightly overlapping at the end of the cast-off
section of the body and sew in place. Place the third
feather above these two feathers and sew in place.

With the 'toes' at the front and using the
photographs for guidance, pin the feet in place on
either side of the gathered cast-off edge. Sew firmly
in place.

P H E A S A N T

# SEAGULL

## Instructions

### BODY AND HEAD

Using white yarn, cast on 14 sts and purl 1 row.
Work increase rows as follows (the first row is written out in full to enable you to see the pattern of the increases):
**Next row:** K1, Kfb, K1, Kfb, Kfb, K1, Kfb, Kfb, K1, Kfb, Kfb, K1, Kfb, K1 (22 sts).
**Next row:** purl.
**Next row:** K1, (Kfb, K3, Kfb) to last st, K1 (30 sts).
**Next row:** purl.
**Next row:** K1, (Kfb, K5, Kfb) to last st, K1 (38 sts).
**Next row:** purl.
**Next row:** K1, (Kfb, K7, Kfb) to last st, K1 (46 sts).
**Next row:** purl.
**Next row:** K1, M1, K21, M1, K2, M1, K21, M1, K1 (50 sts).
**Next row:** purl.
**Next row:** K1, M1, K to last st, M1, K1 (52 sts).
**Next row:** purl.
**Next row:** K1, M1, K24, M1, K2, M1, K24, M1, K1 (56 sts).
Starting with a purl row, work 3 rows in SS.
**Next row:** K25, K2tog, K2, ssK, K25 (54 sts).
**Next row:** purl.
**Next row:** cast off 13 sts, K10, K2tog, K2, ssK, knit to the end of the row (39 sts).
**Next row:** cast off 13 sts, purl to the end of the row (26 sts).
**Next row:** K1, ssK, K7, K2tog, K2, ssK, K7, K2tog, K1 (22 sts).
**Next row:** P1, P2tog, P to last 3 sts, P2togtbl, P1 (20 sts).

**Next row:** K1, ssK, K to last 3 sts, K2tog, K1 (18 sts).
**Next row:** purl.
**Next row:** K1, M1, K7, M1, K2, M1, K7, M1, K1 (22 sts).
**Next row:** purl.
**Next row:** K1, M1, K9, M1, K2, M1, K9, M1, K1 (26 sts).
Starting with a purl row, work 5 rows in SS.
**Next row:** K1, ssK, K7, K2tog, K2, ssK, K7, K2tog, K1 (22 sts).
**Next row:** purl.
**Next row:** K1, ssK, K5, K2tog, K2, ssK, K5, K2tog, K1 (18 sts).
**Next row:** P1, P2tog, P3, P2togtbl, P2, P2tog, P3, P2togtbl, P1 (14 sts).
Divide the remaining sts in half, so that 7 sts are on one needle and 7 sts are on another.
With RS together, fold work in half and cast off using the three-needle cast-off technique (see page 15).

### WING (MAKE TWO)

Using white yarn, cast on 7 sts and work as follows:
**Next row:** Kfb, (P1, K1) twice, P1, Kfb (9 sts).
**Next row:** (K1, P1), four times, K1.
**Next row:** Kfb, (K1, P1) three times, K1, Pfb (11 sts).
Change to grey yarn.
**Next row:** Kfb, (K1, P1) four times, K1, Pfb (13 sts).
**Next row:** (P1, K1) six times, P1.
**Next row:** Pfb, (P1, K1) five times, P1, Kfb (15 sts).
**Next row:** (K1, P1) seven times, K1.
**Next row:** (P1, K1) seven times, P1.
Repeat last 2 rows twice more.
**Next row:** K2tog, (K1, P1) six times, K1 (14 sts).

**Next row:** (P1, K1) six times, K2tog (13 sts).
**Next row:** K2tog, (K1, P1) five times, K1 (12 sts).
**Next row:** (P1, K1) five times, K2tog (11 sts).
**Next row:** K2tog, (K1, P1) four times, K1 (10 sts).
**Next row:** (P1, K1) four times, K2tog (9 sts).
**Next row:** K2tog, (K1, P1) three times, K1 (8 sts).
**Next row:** (P1, K1) three times, K2tog (7 sts).
**Next row:** K2tog, (K1, P1) twice, K1 (6 sts).

## MATERIALS

→ **DK (light worsted/8-ply) yarn:**
   30m (33yd) in white
   10m (11yd) in grey
   10m (11yd) in black
   5m (5½yd) in yellow
→ Two 5mm (¼in) black safety eyes
→ Toy filling

## NEEDLES AND NOTIONS

→ 3mm (US 2 or 3, UK 11) knitting needles and DPN
→ Spare needle
→ Darning needle
→ Sharp scissors
→ Pins

## TENSION

→ 7 sts measured over 2.5cm (1in) and worked in SS using 3mm (US 2 or 3, UK 11) needles

## FINISHED SIZE

→ 14cm (5½in) from top of head to tail

Change to black yarn.
**Next row:** (P1, K1) twice, K2tog (5 sts).
**Next row:** K2tog, K1, P1, K1 (4 sts).
**Next row:** P1, K1, K2tog (3 sts).
**Next row:** K2tog, K1 (2 sts).
**Next row:** K2tog, threading yarn through remaining st to fasten.

## TAIL

Using white yarn, cast on 10 sts and, starting with a knit row, work 3 rows in SS.
Change to grey yarn, and purl 1 row.
**Next row:** K1, ssK, K to last 3 sts, K2tog, K1 (8 sts).
**Next row:** purl.
Repeat last 2 rows once more (6 sts).
Change to black yarn.
**Next row:** K1, ssK, K2tog, K1 (4 sts).
**Next row:** purl.
Knit 3 rows (the second row will form a fold line).
Continuing in SS, and starting with a purl row, work a further 5 rows in SS.
**Next row:** K1, M1, K2, M1, K1 (6 sts).
**Next row:** purl.
**Next row:** K1, M1, K4, M1, K1 (8 sts).
**Next row:** purl.
Cast off.

## FOOT AND LEG (MAKE TWO)

Using yellow yarn, cast on 3 sts and purl 1 row.
**Next row:** (K1, M1) twice, K1 (5 sts)
**Next row:** purl.
**Next row:** K1, M1, K to last st, M1, K1 (7 sts).
**Next row:** purl.

Knit 2 rows (forming a fold line).
Starting with a knit row, work 2 rows in SS.
**Next row:** ssK, K to last 2 sts, K2tog (5 sts).
**Next row:** purl.
Repeat last 2 rows once more (3 sts).
Using DPN and the i-cord technique (see page 12), work 5 rows in SS.
Thread yarn through remaining sts to fasten.

## BEAK

Using yellow yarn and 3mm (US 2 or 3, UK 11) knitting needles, cast on 6 sts.
Starting with a knit row, work 4 rows in SS.
**Next row:** K1, K2tog, ssK, K1 (4 sts).
**Next row:** purl.
Thread yarn through remaining sts, leaving a length of yarn for sewing up.

## MAKING UP

Refer to page 21 for general making up instructions.

Taking the body and starting at the cast-off edge (top of the head), sew the seam along the shaped edge, stopping when you reach the cast-off stitches at the back of the head. Place some toy filling inside the head.

Pin the beak in place, using the photographs for guidance. Thread the safety eyes through the knitting. When you are happy with their placement, remove the Toy filling and beak and push the backs onto the safety eyes to secure them. Re-stuff the head with toy filling. Replace the beak and sew firmly in place.

Continue sewing the seam towards the bottom of the bird until you reach the cast-on edge, stuffing with toy filling as you go. Thread the yarn through the cast-on stitches, gather and secure.

Taking the wings, pin them in place on either side of the back centre seam using the photograph for guidance. Sew each wing in place around the top edges.

Taking the tail piece, fold in half at the fold line and sew the side seams. Place a small amount of toy filling inside the tail. Sew to the body, using the photographs for guidance and stretching out the cast-on edge to fit.

Taking a leg, fold the foot in half at the fold line with WS together. Sew carefully around the edge of the foot. Repeat for the other leg and foot.

Pin the legs in place, either side of the gathered, cast-off edge, using the photographs for guidance. Sew firmly in place.

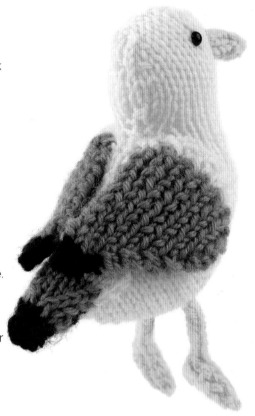

SEAGULL

See page 136 for instructions on making the felt pebbles.

COASTAL BIRDS

# PUFFIN

## Instructions

### BODY AND HEAD

Using white yarn, cast on 14 sts and purl 1 row.
Work increase rows as follows (the first row is written out in full to enable you to see the pattern of the increases):
**Next row:** K1, Kfb, K1, Kfb, Kfb, K1, Kfb, Kfb, K1, Kfb, Kfb, K1, Kfb, K1 (22 sts).
**Next row:** purl.
**Next row:** K1, (Kfb, K3, Kfb) to last st, K1 (30 sts).
**Next row:** purl.
**Next row:** K1, (Kfb, K5, Kfb) to last st, K1 (38 sts).
Get two skeins of black yarn ready so that you can use one at the beginning of the row and one at the end of the row.

## MATERIALS
→ **DK (light worsted/8-ply) yarn:**
  15m (16½yd) in white
  30m (33yd) in black
  1m (1yd) in yellow
  1m (1yd) in red
  1m (1yd) in blue
  5m (5½yd) in orange
→ Two 5mm (¼in) black safety eyes
→ Toy filling

## NEEDLES AND NOTIONS
→ 3mm (US 2 or 3, UK 11) knitting needles and DPN
→ Spare needle
→ Darning needle
→ Sharp scissors
→ Pins

## TENSION
→ 7 sts measured over 2.5cm (1in) and worked in SS using 3mm (US 2 or 3, UK 11) needles

## FINISHED SIZE
→ 11cm (4¼in) from top of head to bottom of the bird

| | BLACK | WHITE | BLACK |
|---|---|---|---|
| NEXT ROW: | P4, | P30, | P4. |
| NEXT ROW: | K1, Kfb, K3, | K4, (Kfb) twice, (K7,Kfb, Kfb) twice, K4, | K3, Kfb, K1 (46 sts). |
| NEXT ROW: | P7, | P32, | P7. |
| NEXT ROW: | K8, | K30, | K8. |
| NEXT ROW: | P8, | P30, | P8. |
| NEXT ROW: | K9, | K28, | K6, w&t. |
| NEXT ROW: | P6, | P28, | P6, w&t. |
| NEXT ROW: | K7, | K26, | K10. |
| NEXT ROW: | P10, | P26, | P10. |
| NEXT ROW: | cast off 3 sts, K7, | K24, | K11 (43 sts). |
| NEXT ROW: | cast off 3 sts, P7, | P24, | P8 (40 sts). |
| NEXT ROW: | K1, ssK, K6, | K22, | K6, K2tog, K1 (38 sts). |
| NEXT ROW: | P8, | P22, | P8. |
| NEXT ROW: | K1, ssK, K6, | K7, K2tog, K2, ssK, K7, | K6, K2tog, K1 (34 sts). |
| NEXT ROW: | P8, | P18, | P8. |
| NEXT ROW: | K1, ssK, K6, | K5, K2tog, K2, ssK, K5, | K6, K2tog, K1 (30 sts). |
| NEXT ROW: | P11, | P8, | P11. |
| NEXT ROW: | K1, ssK, K9, | K2tog, K2, ssK, | K9, K2tog, K1 (26 sts). |

Without breaking off white yarn, continue in black yarn only, as follows:
**Next row:** purl.
**Next row:** K1, ssK, K7, K2tog, K2, ssK, K7, K2tog, K1 (22 sts)
**Next row:** P1, P2tog, P5, P2togtbl, P2, P2tog, P5, P2togtbl, P1 (18 sts)

| | BLACK | WHITE | BLACK |
|---|---|---|---|
| NEXT ROW: | K1, M1, K3, | K4, M1, K2, M1, K4, | K3, M1, K1 (22 sts). |
| NEXT ROW: | P4, | P14, | P4. |
| NEXT ROW: | K1, M1, K2, | K7, M1, K2, M1, K7, | K2, M1, K1 (26 sts). |
| NEXT ROW: | P4, | P18, | P4. |
| NEXT ROW: | K10, | K6, | K10. |

Carrying the black and white yarn along the row, continue as follows to create the eye markings.

| | BLACK | WHITE | BLACK | WHITE | BLACK | WHITE | BLACK |
|---|---|---|---|---|---|---|---|
| NEXT ROW: | P4, | P4, | P2, | P6, | P2, | P4, | P4. |
| NEXT ROW: | K4, | K5, | K1, | K6, | K1, | K5, | K4. |

Continue as follows:

| | BLACK | WHITE | BLACK |
|---|---|---|---|
| **NEXT ROW:** | P4, | P18, | P4. |
| **NEXT ROW:** | K1, ssK, K3, | K4, K2tog, K2, ssK, K4, | K3, K2tog, K1 (22 sts). |
| **NEXT ROW:** | P6, | P10, | P6. |

Break off white yarn and using black yarn, work as follows:
**Next row:** K1, ssK, K5, K2tog, K2, ssK, K5, K2tog, K1 (18 sts).
**Next row:** P1, P2tog, P3, P2togtbl, P2, P2tog, P3, P2togtbl, P1 (14 sts).
Divide the remaining sts in half so that 7 sts are on one needle and 7 sts are on another. With RS together, fold work in half and cast off using the three-needle cast-off technique (see page 15).

## WING (MAKE TWO)

Using black yarn, cast on 7 sts and work as follows:
**Next row:** Kfb, (P1, K1) twice, P1, Kfb (9 sts).
**Next row:** (K1, P1), four times, K1.
**Next row:** Kfb, (K1, P1) three times, K1, Pfb (11 sts).
**Next row:** Kfb, (K1, P1) four times, K1, Pfb (13 sts).
**Next row:** (P1, K1) six times, P1.
**Next row:** Pfb, (P1, K1) five times, P1, Kfb (15 sts).
**Next row:** (K1, P1) seven times, K1.
**Next row:** (P1, K1) seven times, P1.
Repeat last 2 rows twice more.
**Next row:** K2tog, (K1, P1) six times, K1 (14 sts).
**Next row:** (P1, K1) six times, K2tog (13 sts).
**Next row:** K2tog, (K1, P1) five times, K1 (12 sts).
**Next row:** (P1, K1) five times, K2tog (11 sts).
**Next row:** K2tog, (K1, P1) four times, K1 (10 sts).
**Next row:** (P1, K1) four times, K2tog (9 sts).
**Next row:** K2tog, (K1, P1) three times, K1 (8 sts).
**Next row:** (P1, K1) three times, K2tog (7 sts).
**Next row:** K2tog, (K1, P1) twice, K1 (6 sts).
**Next row:** (P1, K1) twice, K2tog (5 sts).
**Next row:** K2tog, K1, P1, K1 (4 sts).
**Next row:** P1, K1, K2tog (3 sts).
**Next row:** K2tog, K1 (2 sts).
**Next row:** K2tog, threading yarn through the remaining st to fasten.

## TAIL

Using black yarn, cast on 10 sts.
Starting with a knit row, work 4 rows in SS.
**Next row:** K1, ssK, K to last 3 sts, K2tog, K1 (8 sts).
**Next row:** purl.
Repeat last 2 rows once more (6 sts).
**Next row:** K1, ssK, K2tog, K1 (4 sts).
Starting with a purl row, work 2 rows in SS.
Knit 3 rows (the second row will form a fold line).
Starting with a purl row, work 5 rows in SS.
**Next row:** K2, M1, K2 (5 sts).
**Next row:** purl.
**Next row:** K1, M1, K3, M1, K1 (7 sts).
**Next row:** purl.
Cast off.

## FOOT AND LEG (MAKE TWO)

Using orange yarn, cast on 3 sts and purl 1 row.
**Next row:** (K1, M1) twice, K1 (5 sts).
**Next row:** purl.
**Next row:** K1, M1, K to last st, M1, K1 (7 sts).
**Next row:** purl.
Knit 2 rows (forming a fold line).
Starting with a knit row, work 2 rows in SS.
**Next row:** ssK, K to last 2 sts, K2tog (5 sts).
**Next row:** purl.
Repeat last 2 rows once more (3 sts).
Using DPN and the i-cord technique (see page 12) work 5 rows in SS.
Thread yarn through remaining sts to fasten.

## BEAK (MAKE TWO HALVES)

Using blue yarn and 3mm (US 2 or 3, UK 11) needles, cast on 7 sts.
**Next row:** K5, w&t.
**Next row:** P3, w&t.
Knit to the end of the row.
Change to yellow yarn and purl 1 row.
Change to red yarn and knit 1 row.
**Next row:** P2tog, P3, P2togtbl (5 sts).
**Next row:** ssK, K1, K2tog (3 sts).
**Next row:** sl1, P2tog, psso.
Thread yarn through remaining st to fasten.

## MAKING UP

Refer to page 21 for general making up instructions.

Taking the body and starting at the cast-off edge (top of the head), sew the seam along the shaped edge, stopping when you reach the cast-off stitches at the back of the head. Place some toy filling inside the head.

Pin the beak in place, using the photographs for guidance. Thread the safety eyes through the knitting. When you are happy with their placement, remove the toy filling and beak and push the backs onto the safety eyes to secure them. Re-stuff the head with toy filling.

With wrong sides facing, carefully sew the beak together, matching the colours. You can use your ends of yarn to stuff the beak. Sew the beak in place with the top and bottom edges meeting the black sections at the top of the head and neck.

Continue sewing the seam towards the bottom of the bird until you reach the cast-on edge, stuffing with toy filling as you go. Thread the yarn through the cast-on stitches, gather and secure.

Taking the wings, pin them in place on either side of the back centre seam using the photograph for guidance. Sew each wing in place around the top edges.

Taking the tail piece, fold in half at the fold line and sew the side seams. Place a small amount of toy filling inside the tail. Sew to the body, using the photographs for guidance and stretching out the cast-on edge to fit.

Taking a leg, fold the foot in half along the fold line with WS together. Sew carefully around the edge of the foot. Repeat for the second leg and foot.

Pin the legs in place, either side of the gathered, cast-off edge, using the photographs for guidance. Sew firmly in place.

PUFFIN

# OYSTERCATCHER

## MATERIALS

→ **DK (light worsted/8-ply) yarn:**
  15m (16½yd) in white
  30m (33yd) in black
  5m (5½yd) in orange

→ Two 5mm (¼in) black safety eyes

→ 2cm (¾in) square of orange felt

→ Toy filling

## NEEDLES AND NOTIONS

→ 3mm (US 2 or 3, UK 11) knitting needles and DPN

→ Spare needle

→ Darning needle

→ Sharp scissors

→ Pins

## TENSION

→ 7 sts measured over 2.5cm (1in) and worked in SS using 3mm (US 2 or 3, UK 11) needles

## FINISHED SIZE

→ 14cm (5½in) from top of head to tail

## Instructions

### BODY AND HEAD

Using white yarn, cast on 14 sts and purl 1 row.
Work increase rows as follows (the first row is written out in full to enable you to see the pattern of the increases):
**Next row:** K1, Kfb, K1, Kfb, Kfb, K1, Kfb, Kfb, K1, Kfb, Kfb, K1, Kfb, K1 (22 sts).
**Next row:** purl.
**Next row:** K1, (Kfb, K3, Kfb) to last st, K1 (30 sts).
**Next row:** purl.
**Next row:** K1, (Kfb, K5, Kfb) to last st, K1 (38 sts).
**Next row:** purl.
**Next row:** K1, (Kfb, K7, Kfb) to last st, K1 (46 sts).
**Next row:** purl.
**Next row:** K1, M1, K21, M1, K2, M1, K21, M1, K1 (50 sts).
**Next row:** purl.
**Next row:** K1, M1, K to last st, M1, K1 (52 sts).
**Next row:** purl.
**Next row:** K1, M1, K24, M1, K2, M1, K24, M1, K1 (56 sts).
**Next row:** purl.
Join in black yarn and work as follows:
I used three separate mini balls of black yarn so that it didn't show through on the right side.

| NEXT ROW: | BLACK | WHITE | BLACK | WHITE | BLACK |
|---|---|---|---|---|---|
| NEXT ROW: | K4, | K22, | K4, | K22, | K4. |
| NEXT ROW: | P5, | P20, | P6, | P20, | P5. |
| NEXT ROW: | K14, | K9, | K2, ssK, K2, K2tog, K2, | K9, | K14 (54 sts). |
| NEXT ROW: | P15, | P7, | P10, | P7, | P15. |
| NEXT ROW: | cast off 13 sts, K2, | K5, | K3, ssK, K2, K2tog, K3, | K5, | K16 (39 sts). |
| NEXT ROW: | cast off 13 sts, P3, | P3, | P12, | P3, | P4 (26 sts). |

Break off white yarn and using black yarn only work as follows:
**Next row:** K1, ssK, K7, K2tog, K2, ssK, K7, K2tog, K1 (22 sts).
**Next row:** P1, P2tog, P to last 3 sts, P2togtbl, P1 (20 sts).
**Next row:** K1, ssK, K to last 3 sts, K2tog, K1 (18 sts).
**Next row:** purl.
**Next row:** K1, M1, K7, M1, K2, M1, K7, M1, K1 (22 sts).
**Next row:** purl.
**Next row:** K1, M1, K9, M1, K2, M1, K9, M1, K1 (26 sts).
Starting with a purl row, work 5 rows in SS.
**Next row:** K1, ssK, K7, K2tog, K2, ssK, K7, K2tog, K1 (22 sts).
**Next row:** purl.
**Next row:** K1, ssK, K5, K2tog, K2, ssK, K5, K2tog, K1 (18 sts).
**Next row:** P1, P2tog, P3, P2togtbl, P2, P2tog, P3, P2togtbl, P1 (14 sts).
Divide the remaining sts in half, so that 7 sts are on one needle and 7 sts are on another. With RS together, fold work in half and cast off using the three-needle cast-off technique (see page 15).

## WING (MAKE TWO)

Using black yarn, cast on 7 sts and work as follows:
**Next row:** Kfb, (P1, K1) twice, P1, Kfb (9 sts).
**Next row:** (K1, P1), four times, K1.
**Next row:** Kfb, (K1, P1) three times, K1, Pfb (11 sts).
**Next row:** Kfb, (K1, P1) four times, K1, Pfb (13 sts).
**Next row:** (P1, K1) six times, P1.
**Next row:** Pfb, (P1, K1) five times, P1, Kfb (15 sts).

**Next row:** (K1, P1) seven times, K1.
**Next row:** (P1, K1) seven times, P1.
Repeat last 2 rows twice more.
**Next row:** K2tog, (K1, P1) six times, K1 (14 sts).
**Next row:** (P1, K1) six times, K2tog (13 sts).
**Next row:** K2tog, (K1, P1) five times, K1 (12 sts).
**Next row:** (P1, K1) five times, K2tog (11 sts).
**Next row:** K2tog, (K1, P1) four times, K1 (10 sts).
**Next row:** (P1, K1) four times, K2tog (9 sts).
**Next row:** K2tog, (K1, P1) three times, K1 (8 sts).
**Next row:** (P1, K1) three times, K2tog (7 sts).
**Next row:** K2tog, (K1, P1) twice, K1 (6 sts).
**Next row:** (P1, K1) twice, K2tog (5 sts).
**Next row:** K2tog, K1, P1, K1 (4 sts).
**Next row:** P1, K1, K2tog (3 sts).
**Next row:** K2tog, K1 (2 sts).
**Next row:** K2tog, threading yarn through remaining st to fasten.

## TAIL

Using black yarn, cast on 5 sts and, starting with a knit row, work 4 rows in SS.
**Next row:** ssK, K1, K2tog (3 sts).
Starting with a purl row, work 3 rows in SS.
Knit 3 rows (the second row will form a fold line).
Starting with a purl row, work 3 rows in SS.
**Next row:** (K1, M1) twice, K1 (5 sts).
**Next row:** purl.
Cast off.

## FOOT AND LEG (MAKE TWO)

Using orange yarn, cast on 3 sts and purl 1 row.
**Next row:** (K1, M1) twice, K1 (5 sts).
**Next row:** purl.
**Next row:** K1, M1, K to last st, M1, K1 (7 sts).
**Next row:** purl.
Knit 2 rows (forming a fold line).
Starting with a knit row, work 2 rows in SS.
**Next row:** ssK, K to last 2 sts, K2tog (5 sts).
**Next row:** purl.
Repeat last 2 rows once more (3 sts).
Using DPN and the i-cord technique work five rows in SS.
Thread yarn through remaining sts to fasten.

## BEAK

Using orange yarn and 3mm (US 2 or 3, UK 11) knitting needles, cast on 5 sts.
**Next row:** K2, sl1, K2.
**Next row:** purl.
Repeat last 2 rows three more times.

**Next row:** ssK, K1, K2tog (3 sts).
**Next row:** purl.
**Next row:** CDD (1 st).
Thread yarn through remaining st, leaving a length of yarn for sewing up.

## MAKING UP

First, follow the instructions on page 20 for mounting the safety eyes onto the felt backing and refer to page 21 for general making up instructions.

Taking the body and starting at the cast-off edge (top of the head), sew the seam along the shaped edge, stopping when you reach the cast-off stitches at the back of the head. Place some toy filling inside the head.

Pin the beak in place, using the photographs for guidance. Thread the safety eyes through the knitting. When you are happy with their position, remove the toy filling and beak and push the backs onto the safety eyes to secure them. Re-stuff the head with toy filling. Replace the beak and sew firmly in place.

Continue sewing the seam towards the bottom of the bird until you reach the cast-on edge, stuffing with toy filling as you go. Thread the yarn through the cast-on stitches, gather and secure.

Taking the wings, pin them in place on either side of the back centre seam using the photograph for guidance. Sew each wing in place around the top edges.

Taking the tail piece, fold in half along the fold line and sew the side seams. Place a small amount of toy filling inside the tail. Sew to the body, using the photographs for guidance and stretching out the cast-on edge to fit.

Taking a leg, fold the foot in half along the fold line with WS together. Sew carefully around the edge of the foot. Repeat for the second leg and foot.

Pin the legs in place, either side of the gathered, cast-off edge, using the photographs for guidance. Sew firmly in place.

# FLAMINGO

## Instructions

### BODY AND HEAD

Using pink yarn, cast on 14 sts and purl 1 row.
Work increase rows as follows (the first row is
written out in full to enable you to see the pattern
of the increases):
**Next row:** K1, Kfb, K1, Kfb, Kfb, K1, Kfb, Kfb, K1, Kfb,
Kfb, K1, Kfb, K1 (22 sts).
**Next row:** purl.
**Next row:** K1, (Kfb, K3, Kfb) to last st, K1 (30 sts).
**Next row:** purl.
**Next row:** K1, (Kfb, K5, Kfb) to last st, K1 (38 sts).
**Next row:** purl.
**Next row:** K1, (Kfb, K7, Kfb) to last st, K1 (46 sts).
**Next row:** purl.
**Next row:** K1, M1, K21, M1, K2, M1, K21, M1, K1 (50 sts).
Starting with a purl row, work 3 rows in SS.
**Next row:** K24, M1, K2, M1, K24 (52 sts).
Starting with a purl row work 3 rows in SS.
**Next row:** K16, w&t.
**Next row:** P13, w&t.
**Next row:** K11, w&t.
**Next row:** P9, w&t.
**Next row:** knit to the end of row.
**Next row:** P16, w&t.
**Next row:** K13, w&t.
**Next row:** P11, w&t.
**Next row:** K9, w&t.
**Next row:** purl to the end of row.
Cast off 17 sts at the beginning of the next 2 rows
(18 sts).
**Next row:** K1, ssK, K11, w&t.
**Next row:** P9, w&t.
**Next row:** K to last 3 sts, K2tog, K1 (16 sts).
**Next row:** purl.
**Next row:** K14, w&t.
**Next row:** P12, w&t.
**Next row:** K11 w&t.
**Next row:** P10, w&t.
**Next row:** knit to the end of row.
**Next row:** purl.
**Next row:** K1, ssK, K9, w&t.

**Next row:** P8, w&t.
**Next row:** knit to last 3 sts, K2tog, K1 (14 sts).
**Next row:** purl.
**Next row:** K1, ssK, K to last 3 sts, K2tog, K1 (12 sts).
**Next row:** purl.
*Next row: K5, w&t.
**Next row:** purl to the end of row.
**Next row:** K4, w&t.
**Next row:** purl to the end of row.
**Next row:** K3, w&t.
**Next row:** purl to the end of row.
**Next row:** knit.
**Next row:** P5, w&t.
**Next row:** knit to the end of row.
**Next row:** P4, w&t.
**Next row:** knit to the end of row.

### MATERIALS
→ **DK (light worsted/8-ply) yarn:**
　30m (33yd) in pink
　10m (11yd) in bright coral
　10m (11yd) in light coral
　1m (1yd) in black
　1m (1yd) in white
→ Two 5mm (¼in) black safety eyes
→ Toy filling

### NEEDLES AND NOTIONS
→ 3mm (US 2 or 3, UK 11) knitting needles
　and DPN
→ Darning needle for sewing up
→ sharp scissors

### TENSION
→ 7 sts measured over 2.5cm (1in) and worked in
　SS using 3mm (US 2 or 3, UK 11) needles

### FINISHED SIZE
→ 12cm (4¾in) from top of head to bottom of body

**Next row:** P3, w&t.
**Next row:** knit to the end of row.
**Next row:** purl.*
Repeat from * to * once more.
**Next row:** K4, w&t.
**Next row:** purl. to the end of row.
**Next row:** K3, w&t.
**Next row:** purl. to the end of row.
**Next row:** K2, w&t.
**Next row:** purl to the end of row.
**Next row:** knit.
**Next row:** P4, w&t.
**Next row:** knit to the end of row.
**Next row:** P3, w&t.
**Next row:** knit to the end of row.
**Next row:** P2, w&t.
**Next row:** knit to the end of row.
**Next row:** purl.
**Next row:** K1, M1, K4, M1, K2, M1, K4, M1, K1 (16 sts).
**Next row:** P7, M1, P2, M1, P7 (18 sts).
**Next row:** K8, M1, K2, M1, K8 (20 sts).
Starting with a purl row, work 3 rows in SS.
**Next row:** K1, ssK, K4, K2tog, K2, ssK, K4, K2tog, K1 (16 sts).
**Next row:** P1, P2tog, P2, P2togtbl, P2, P2tog, P2, P2togtbl, P1 (12 sts).
**Next row:** K1, ssK, K2tog, K2, ssK, K2tog, K1 (8 sts).
Thread yarn through remaining sts and gather, leaving a length of yarn for sewing up.

## WING (MAKE TWO)

Using light coral yarn, cast on 7 sts.
**Next row:** Kfb, (K1, P1) twice, K1, Kfb (9 sts).
**Next row:** Kfb, (K1, P1) three times, K1, Kfb (11 sts).
**Next row:** Kfb, (K1, P1) four times, K1, Kfb (13 sts).
**Next row:** (P1, K1) six times, P1.
**Next row:** (K1, P1) six times, K1.
Repeat last 2 rows twice more.
**Next row:** (P1, K1) six times, P1.
**Next row:** K2tog, (K1, P1) five times, K1 (12 sts).
**Next row:** (P1, K1) five times, K2tog (11 sts).
**Next row:** K2tog, (K1, P1) four times, K1 (10 sts).
**Next row:** (P1, K1) four times, K2tog (9 sts).
**Next row:** K2tog, (K1, P1) twice, K1, K2tog (7 sts).
**Next row:** K2tog, K1, P1, K1, K2tog (5 sts).
**Next row:** K2tog, K1, K2tog (3 sts).
**Next row:** CDD (1 st).
Thread yarn through remaining st to fasten.

## FOOT AND LEG (MAKE TWO)

Using bright coral yarn, cast on 3 sts and purl 1 row.
**Next row:** (K1, M1) twice, K1 (5 sts).
**Next row:** purl.
**Next row:** K1, M1, K to last st, M1, K1 (7 sts).
**Next row:** purl.
Knit 2 rows (forming a fold line).
Starting with a knit row, work 2 rows in SS.
**Next row:** ssK, K to last 2 sts, K2tog (5 sts).
**Next row:** purl.
Repeat last two rows once more (3 sts).
Using DPN and the i-cord technique (see page 12), work in SS until leg measures 8cm (3¼in).
Thread yarn through remaining sts and fasten.
Tie a knot in the leg to make the knee, using the photograph as guidance.

## BEAK

Using white yarn and 3mm (US 2 or 3, UK 11) knitting needles, cast on 7 sts.
**Next row:** sl1, K2, sl1, K2, turn work (leaving 1 st unworked).
**Next row:** purl to last st, sl1 (7 sts).
Change to black yarn.
**Next row:** K3, sl1, K3.
**Next row:** purl.
**Next row:** K3, sl1, K3.
**Next row:** P1, P2tog, P1, P2togtbl, P1 (5 sts).
**Next row:** ssK, K1, K2tog (3 sts).
**Next row:** CDD (1 st).
Thread yarn through remaining st, leaving a length of yarn for sewing up.

## MAKING UP

Refer to page 21 for general making up instructions.
  Taking the body and starting at the cast-off edge (top of the head), sew the seam along the shaped edge, stopping when you reach the back of the head. Place some toy filling inside the head.
  Sew the seam on the beak and pin in place, using the photographs for guidance. Thread the safety eyes through the knitting (see page 21). When you are happy with their position, remove the toy filling and beak and push the backs onto the safety eyes to secure them. Re-stuff the head with toy filling.
  Continue sewing the seam, stuffing the neck with toy filling as you go. Continue sewing the seam along the back of the bird until you reach the cast-on edge, stuffing with toy filling as you go. Thread the yarn through the cast-on stitches, gather and secure. Replace the beak and sew firmly in place.
  Taking the wings, pin in place on the body with the sloped edge at the top and using the photographs for guidance. Sew each one in place, stuffing with a small amount of toy filling to give definition.

# PARAKEET

## Instructions

### BODY AND HEAD

Using mid green yarn, cast on 14 sts and purl 1 row. Work increase rows as follows: (the first row is written out in full to enable you to see the pattern of the increases):

**Next row:** K1, Kfb, K1, Kfb, Kfb, K1, Kfb, Kfb, K1, Kfb, Kfb, K1, Kfb, K1 (22 sts).

**Next row:** purl.

**Next row:** K1, (Kfb, K3, Kfb) to last st, K1 (30 sts).

**Next row:** purl.

**Next row:** K1, (Kfb, K5, Kfb) to last st, K1 (38 sts).

**Next row:** purl.

**Next row:** K1, M1, K17, M1, K2, M1, K17, M1, K1 (42 sts). Starting with a purl row, work 3 rows in SS.

**Next row:** cast off 3 sts, K35, w&t (39 sts).

**Next row:** P33, w&t.

Knit to the end of the row.

**Next row:** cast off 3 sts, purl to the end of the row (36 sts). Starting with a knit row, work 2 rows in SS.

**Next row:** K1, ssK, K to last 3 sts, K2tog, K1 (34 sts).

**Next row:** purl.

**Next row:** K1, ssK, K11, K2tog, K2, ssK, K11, K2tog, K1 (30 sts).

**Next row:** purl.

**Next row:** K1, ssK, K9, K2tog, K2, ssK, K9, K2tog, K1 (26 sts).

**Next row:** purl.

**Next row:** K1, ssK, K7, K2tog, K2, ssK, K7, K2tog, K1 (22 sts).

**Next row:** P1, P2tog, P5, P2togtbl, P2, P2tog, P5, P2togtbl, P1 (18 sts).

**Next row:** K1, M1, K7, M1, K2, M1, K7, M1, K1 (22 sts).

**Next row:** P1, M1, P9, M1, P2, M1, P9, M1, P1 (26 sts). Starting with a knit row, work 6 rows in SS.

**Next row:** K1, ssK, K7, K2tog, K2, ssK, K7, K2tog, K1 (22 sts).

**Next row:** P1, P2tog, P5, P2togtbl, P2, P2tog, P5, P2togtbl, P1 (18 sts).

**Next row:** K1, ssK, K3, K2tog, K2, ssK, K3, K2tog, K1 (14 sts).

### MATERIALS

→ **DK (light worsted/8-ply) yarn:**
   30m (33yd) in mid green
   20m (22yd) in dark green
   10m (11yd) in orange
   1m (1yd) in red
   1m (1yd) in black
→ Two 5mm (¼in) black safety eyes
→ 2cm (¾in) square of red felt
→ Toy filling

### NEEDLES AND NOTIONS

→ 3mm (US 2 or 3, UK 11) knitting needles and DPN
→ Darning needle for sewing up
→ Sharp scissors
→ Pins

### TENSION

→ 7 sts measured over 2.5cm (1in) and worked in SS using 3mm (US 2 or 3, UK 11) needles

### FINISHED SIZE

→ 10cm (4in) from top of head to bottom of body

Divide the remaining sts in half, so that 7 sts are on one needle and 7 sts are on another.

With RS together, fold work in half and cast off using the three-needle cast-off technique (see page 15).

### WING (MAKE TWO)

Using dark green yarn, cast on 7 sts and work as follows:

**Next row:** Kfb, (P1, K1) twice, P1, Kfb (9 sts).

**Next row:** (K1, P1) four times, K1.

**Next row:** Kfb, (K1, P1) three times, K1, Pfb (11 sts).

**Next row:** Kfb, (K1, P1) four times, K1, Pfb (13 sts).

**Next row:** (P1, K1) six times, P1.

**Next row:** Pfb, (P1, K1) five times, P1, Kfb (15 sts).

**Next row:** (K1, P1) seven times, K1.
**Next row:** (P1, K1) seven times, P1.
Repeat last 2 rows twice more.
**Next row:** K2tog, (K1, P1) six times, K1 (14 sts).
**Next row:** (P1, K1) six times, K2tog (13 sts).
**Next row:** K2tog, (K1, P1) five times, K1 (12 sts).
**Next row:** (P1, K1) five times, K2tog (11 sts).
**Next row:** K2tog, (K1, P1) four times, K1 (10 sts).
**Next row:** (P1, K1) four times, K2tog (9 sts).
**Next row:** K2tog, (K1, P1) three times, K1 (8 sts).
**Next row:** (P1, K1) three times, K2tog (7 sts).
**Next row:** K2tog, (K1, P1) twice, K1 (6 sts).
**Next row:** (P1, K1) twice, K2tog (5 sts).
**Next row:** K2tog, K1, P1, K1 (4 sts).
**Next row:** P1, K1, K2tog (3 sts).
**Next row:** K2tog, K1 (2 sts).
**Next row:** K2tog, threading yarn through remaining st to fasten.

## TAIL FEATHER

Make two in dark green and one in mid green.
Cast on 7 sts and work as follows:
**Next row:** K3, sl1, K3.
**Next row:** purl.
Repeat last 2 rows four more times.
**Next row:** K1, ssk, sl1, K2tog, K1 (5 sts).
**Next row:** purl.
**Next row:** K2, sl1, K2.
**Next row:** purl.
Repeat last 2 rows three more times.
**Next row:** ssK, sl1, k2tog (3 sts).
**Next row:** purl.
**Next row:** CDD (1 st).
Thread yarn through remaining st
to fasten.

## FOOT (MAKE TWO)

Using orange yarn and DPN, cast on 6 sts.
**Next row:** cast off 4 sts, K1 (2 sts).
**\*Next row:** K2.
**Next row:** cast on 4 sts, cast off 4 sts, K1 (2 sts)\*.
Work from \* to \* once more to make a third toe,
casting off 5 sts on the last row (1 st).
With RS facing, pick up and knit 2 sts across the top
of the toes (3 sts).
Work 3 rows in SS using the i-cord technique (see
page 12). Thread yarn through sts, leaving a length
of yarn for sewing up.

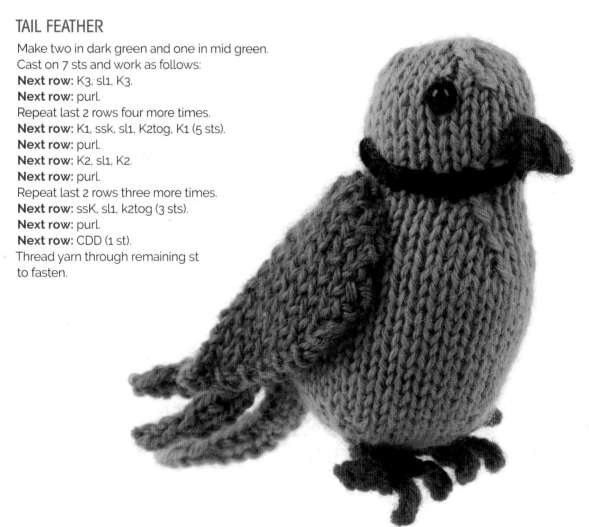

## BEAK

Using orange yarn and 3mm (US 2 or 3, UK 11) needles, cast on 7 sts and knit 1 row.
**Next row:** P2tog, P3, P2togtbl (5 sts).
Starting with a knit row, work 2 rows in SS.
**Next row:** K1, CDD, K1 (3 sts).
**Next row:** sl1, P2tog, psso (1 st).
Thread yarn through remaining st to fasten.

## MAKING UP

First, follow the instructions on page 20 for mounting the safety eyes onto the felt backing and refer to page 21 for general making up instructions.

Taking the body and starting at the cast off edge (top of the head), sew the seam along the shaped edge, stopping when you reach the cast-off stitches at the back of the head. Place some toy filling inside the head.

Sew the seam on the beak and pin in place, using the photographs for guidance. Thread the safety eyes through the knitting. When you are happy with their position, remove the toy filling and beak and push the backs onto the safety eyes to secure them. Re-stuff the head with toy filling. Replace the beak and sew firmly in place. Continue sewing the seam along the back of the bird until you reach the cast-on edge, stuffing with toy filling as you go. Thread the yarn through the cast-on stitches, gather and secure.

Taking the three tail feathers, sew the seam along the length of each one. Pin two feathers in place slightly overlapping at the end of the cast-off section of the body and sew in place. Place the third feather below these two feathers and sew in place.

Using black yarn, embroider a line of chain stitch along the neck, using the photographs for guidance. Using red yarn, embroider a line of straight stitches above this. If it helps, mark the line first using sewing cotton as a guide. You can then pull this out after the embroidery is done.

# HUMMINGBIRD

## Instructions

### BODY AND HEAD

Note: you will be using all 6 strands of the metallic embroidery yarn together.

Using magenta yarn, cast on 14 sts and purl 1 row.
Work increase rows as follows (the first row is written out in full to enable you to see the pattern of the increases):
**Next row:** K1, Kfb, K1, Kfb, Kfb, K1, Kfb, Kfb, K1, Kfb, Kfb, K1, Kfb, K1 (22 sts).
**Next row:** purl.
**Next row:** K1, (Kfb, K3, Kfb) to last st, K1 (30 sts).
Join in metallic thread and also use two mini balls of magenta yarn at each side to avoid carrying the yarn across the back of the work. Knot the beginning of the thread to stop it fraying.

## MATERIALS

→ **DK (light worsted/8-ply) yarn:**
   10m (11yd) in magenta
   10m (11yd) in purple
   1m (1yd) in black
→ 8m (8¾yd) skein of metallic embroidery thread
→ Two 5mm (¼in) black safety eyes
→ Toy filling

## NEEDLES AND NOTIONS

→ 3mm (US 2 or 3, UK 11) knitting needles
→ 2.5mm (US 1 or 2, UK 12 or 13) DPN
→ Darning needle for sewing up
→ sharp scissors

## TENSION

→ 7 sts measured over 2.5cm (1in) and worked in SS using 3mm (US 2 or 3, UK 11) needles

## FINISHED SIZE

→ 9cm (3½in) from top of head to tail

| | MAGENTA | METALLIC EMBROIDERY THREAD | MAGENTA |
|---|---|---|---|
| **NEXT ROW:** | P11, | P8, | P11. |
| **NEXT ROW:** | K10, | K4, M1, K2, M1, K4, | K10 (32 sts). |
| **NEXT ROW:** | P8, | P16, | P8. |
| **NEXT ROW:** | K6, | K20, | K6. |
| **NEXT ROW:** | P5, | P22, | P5. |
| **NEXT ROW:** | Cast off 2 sts, K1, | K24, | K4 (30 sts). |
| **NEXT ROW:** | Cast off 2 sts, P1, | P24, | P2 (28 sts). |
| **NEXT ROW:** | K2, | K24, | K2. |
| **NEXT ROW:** | P2, | P24, | P2. |
| **NEXT ROW:** | K2, | ssK, K20, K2tog, | K2 (26 sts). |
| **NEXT ROW:** | P2, | P22, | P2. |
| **NEXT ROW:** | K2, | ssK, K18, K2tog, | K2 (24 sts). |
| **NEXT ROW:** | P2, | P20, | P2. |
| **NEXT ROW:** | K2, | ssK, K16, K2tog, | K2 (22 sts). |
| **NEXT ROW:** | P2, | P18, | P2. |
| **NEXT ROW:** | K2, | ssK, K4, K2tog, K2, ssK, K4, K2tog, | K2 (18 sts). |
| **NEXT ROW:** | P2, | P2tog, P2, P2togtbl, P2, P2tog, P2, P2togtbl, | P2 (14 sts). |

Break off metallic embroidery thread and using
magenta yarn continue as follows:
**Next row:** knit.
**Next row:** P1, M1, P5, M1, P2, M1, P5, M1, P1 (18 sts).
**Next row:** K8, M1, K2, M1, K8 (20 sts).
Starting with a purl row, work 4 rows in SS.
Change to purple yarn and purl 1 row.
**Next row:** K1, ssK, K4, K2tog, K2, ssK, K4, K2tog, K1
(16 sts).
**Next row:** purl.
**Next row:** K1, ssK, K2, K2tog, K2, ssK, K2, K2tog, K1
(12 sts).
**Next row:** P1, P2tog, P2togtbl, P2, P2tog, P2togbtl, P1
(8 sts).
**Next row:** (K2tog) four times (4 sts).
Thread yarn through remaining sts, leaving a length
of yarn for sewing up.

## WING (MAKE TWO)

Using purple yarn, cast on 7 sts and work as follows:
**Next row:** (P1, K1) three times, P1.
**Next row:** (K1, P1) three times, K1.
Repeat last 2 rows once more.
**Next row:** Kfb, (K1, P1) three times (8 sts).
**Next row:** (K1, P1) four times.
**Next row:** Kfb, (P1, K1) three times, P1 (9 sts).
**Next row:** K2tog, (K1, P1) three times, K1 (8 sts).
**Next row:** (P1, K1) four times.
Repeat last row once more.
**Next row:** (P1, K1) three times, K2tog (7 sts).
**Next row:** (K1, P1) three times, K1.
**Next row:** K2tog, (P1, K1) twice, P1 (6 sts).
**Next row:** K2tog, K1, P1, K2tog (4 sts).
**Next row:** (P1, K1) twice.
Repeat last row twice more.
**Next row:** (K2tog) twice (2 sts).
**Next row:** K2tog (1 st).
Fasten off remaining stitch.

## TAIL

Using magenta yarn, cast on 5 sts.
Starting with a knit row, work 8 rows in SS.
Cast off, leaving a length of yarn for sewing up.

## BEAK

Using black yarn and 2.5mm (US 1 or 2, UK 12 or 13) DPN, cast on 4 sts.
Using the i-cord technique (see page 12) throughout, work 5 rows in SS.

**Next row:** K1, K2tog, K1 (3 sts).
Work 3 rows in SS.
Thread yarn through remaining sts to fasten.

## MAKING UP

Refer to page 21 for general making up instructions.

Taking the body and starting at the cast off edge (top of the head), sew the seam along the shaped edge, stopping when you reach the cast-off stitches at the back of the head. Place some toy filling inside the head.

Sew the seam on the beak and pin in place, using the photographs for guidance. Thread the safety eyes through the knitting. When you are happy with their placement, remove the toy filling and beak and push the backs onto the safety eyes to secure them. Re-stuff the head with toy filling. Replace the beak and sew firmly in place.

Continue sewing the seam along the back of the bird until you reach the cast-on edge, stuffing with Toy filling as you go. Thread the yarn through the cast-on stitches, gather and secure.

Taking the tail piece, sew the cast-on edge to the body by approximately 1cm (½in), covering the cast-off stitches of the body. Fold the rest of the tail lengthwise and sew the seam together.

Sew the wings in place along the join between the metallic embroidery thread and the magenta yarn, using the photographs for guidance. Embroider two feet using black yarn and straight stitches. See the photograph of the crossbill's feet on page 117 for guidance.

# WREN

## Instructions

### BODY AND HEAD

Using beige yarn, cast on 14 sts and purl 1 row.
Work increase rows as follows (the first row is written out in full to enable you to see the pattern of the increases):
**Next row (RS):** K1, Kfb, K1, Kfb, Kfb, K1, Kfb, Kfb, K1, Kfb, Kfb, K1, Kfb, K1 (22 sts).
**Next row:** purl.
**Next row:** K1, (Kfb, K3, Kfb) to last st, K1 (30 sts).
Starting with a purl row, work 9 rows in SS.
**Next row:** K3, w&t.
**Next row:** purl to the end of the row.
**Next row:** K14, M1, K2, M1, K14 (32 sts).
**Next row:** P3, w&t.
**Next row:** knit to the end of the row.
**Next row:** purl.
Join in red brown yarn and work as follows:

| | RED BROWN | BEIGE | RED BROWN |
|---|---|---|---|
| **NEXT ROW:** | K6, | K20, | K6. |
| **NEXT ROW:** | P8, | P16, | P8. |
| **NEXT ROW:** | K12, | K8, | K12. |
| **NEXT ROW:** | P13, | P6, | P13. |
| **NEXT ROW:** | cast off 6 sts, K7, | K4, | K14 (26 sts). |
| **NEXT ROW:** | working all sts in red brown yarn, cast off 6 sts, purl to end of row (20 sts). | | |
| **NEXT ROW:** | working all sts in red brown yarn, cast off 3 sts, knit to end of row (17 sts). | | |
| **NEXT ROW:** | cast off 3 sts, | P12, | P1 (14 sts). |

Break off beige yarn and continue using red brown yarn only.
**Next row:** K1, ssK, K1, K2tog, K2, ssK, K1, K2tog, K1 (10 sts).
**Next row:** purl.
**Next row:** (K2tog) five times (5 sts).
Thread yarn through remaining sts to fasten.

## WING (MAKE TWO)

Using red brown yarn, cast on 5 sts and work as follows:
**Next row:** (P1, K1) twice, P1.
**Next row:** Kfb, P1, K1, Pfb, K1 (7 sts).
**Next row:** (P1, K2) twice, P1.
**Next row:** (K1, Pfb, P1) twice, Kfb (10 sts).
**Next row:** Kfb, (P1, K1) four times, Pfb (12 sts).
**Next row:** (P1, K1) six times.
Repeat last row four more times.
**Next row:** cast off 2 sts, (K1, P1) four times, K1 (10 sts).
**Next row:** (P1, K1) five times.
**Next row:** cast off 2 sts, (K1, P1) twice, K1, P2tog (7 sts).
**Next row:** (K1, P1) three times, K1.
**Next row:** cast off 2 sts, K1, P1, K2tog (4 sts).
**Next row:** (P1, K1) twice.
**Next row:** cast off 2 sts, K1 (2 sts).
**Next row:** K2tog, threading yarn through remaining st to fasten.

## TAIL

Using red brown yarn, cast on 5 sts. Starting with a knit row, work 2 rows in SS.
**Next row:** K1, CDD, K1 (3 sts).
Starting with a purl row, work 7 rows in SS.
Purl 2 rows (the first row will form a fold line).
Starting with a knit row, work 6 rows in SS.
Cast off.

## BEAK

Using dark brown yarn and 2.5mm (US 1 or 2, UK 12 or 13) needles, cast on 4 sts and purl 1 row.
**Next row:** ssK, K2tog (2 sts).
**Next row:** P2tog (1 st).
Thread yarn through remaining st to fasten, leaving a length of yarn for sewing up.

## MAKING UP

Refer to page 21 for general making up instructions.

Taking the body and starting at the cast-off edge (top of the head), sew the seam, stopping when you reach the cast-off stitches at the back of the head. Place some toy filling inside the head – this will enable you to see exactly how the eyes look before you secure them. Taking the beak, sew the side seam and pin in place, approximately level with the cast-off stitches along the back of the bird.

Thread the eyes through the knitting, using the photographs for guidance. Remove the toy filling and beak and push the backs onto the safety eyes to secure them. Re-stuff the head with toy filling. Replace the beak and sew firmly in place.

Continue sewing the seam along the back of the bird until you reach the cast-on edge, stuffing with Toy filling as you go. Thread the yarn through the cast-on stitches, gather and secure.

Taking the wings, pin them in place on either side of the back centre seam using the photographs for guidance. Sew each wing in place along the front edge and for approximately 2cm (¾in) along the top edge.

Taking the tail, with wrong sides together fold along the fold line and sew the seams. Note that one side of the tail is shorter than the other. Pin in place on the body with the longer side overlapping the back of the bird so that the tail points upwards. Sew in place.

Using dark brown yarn and straight stitches, embroider a foot either side of the centre stitches at the base of the bird. See the photograph of the crossbill's feet on page 117 for guidance.

# BULLFINCH

## Instructions

### BODY AND HEAD

Using cream yarn, cast on 14 sts and purl 1 row.
Work increase rows as follows: (the first row is
written out in full to enable you to see the pattern of
the increases):
**Next row (RS):** K1, Kfb, K1, Kfb, Kfb, K1, Kfb, Kfb, K1, Kfb,
Kfb, K1, Kfb, K1 (22 sts).
**Next row:** purl.
**Next row:** K1, (Kfb, K3, Kfb) to last st, K1 (30 sts).

|  | CREAM | CORAL | CREAM |
|---|---|---|---|
| **NEXT ROW:** | P11, | P8, | P11. |
| **NEXT ROW:** | K1, Kfb, K4, | K1, (Kfb) twice, K5, (Kfb) twice, K5, (Kfb) twice, K1, | K4, Kfb, K1 (38 sts). |
| **NEXT ROW:** | P3, | P32, | P3. |

Break off cream yarn and continue using coral yarn only.
**Next row:** K1, (Kfb, K7, Kfb) to last st, K1 (46 sts).
Starting with a purl row, work 9 rows in SS.

|  | CORAL | LIGHT GREY | CORAL | LIGHT GREY | CORAL |
|---|---|---|---|---|---|
| **NEXT ROW:** | Cast off 4 sts, | K9, | K18, | K9, | K5 (42 sts). |
| **NEXT ROW:** | Cast off 4 sts, | P10, | P16, | P11 (38 sts). | (no stitches) |

## MATERIALS

→ **DK (light worsted/8-ply) yarn:**
    20m (22yd) light grey
    20m (22yd) coral
    2m (2yd) dark grey
    10m (11 yd) cream
    10m (11 yd) black
→ Two 5mm (¼in) black safety eyes
→ Toy filling

## NEEDLES AND NOTIONS

→ 3mm (US 2 or 3, UK 11)
    knitting needles and DPN
→ Darning needle
→ Sharp scissors
→ Pins

## TENSION

→ 7 sts measured over 2.5cm (1in)
    and worked in SS using 3mm
    (US 2 or 3, UK 11) needles

## FINISHED SIZE

→ 11cm (4¼in) from beak to tail

From now on you will only use the coral yarn in the middle of the row.

|  | LIGHT GREY | CORAL | LIGHT GREY |
|---|---|---|---|
| **NEXT ROW:** | cast off 6 sts, K5, | K5, ssK, K2tog, K5, | K12 (30 sts). |
| **NEXT ROW:** | cast off 6 sts, P6, | P4, M1, P2, M1, P4, | P7 (26 sts). |

Join in black yarn and work as follows:

|  | LIGHT GREY | CORAL | BLACK | CORAL | LIGHT GREY |
|---|---|---|---|---|---|
| **NEXT ROW:** | K1, ssK, K4, | K5, | K2, | K5, | K4, K2tog, K1 (24 sts). |
| **NEXT ROW:** | P1, P2tog, P1, | P6, | P4, | P6, | P1, P2togtbl, P1 (22 sts). |

Break off light grey yarn and work as follows:

|  | BLACK | CORAL | BLACK | CORAL | BLACK |
|---|---|---|---|---|---|
| **NEXT ROW:** | K3, | K5, | K6, | K5, | K3. |
| **NEXT ROW:** | P3, | P4, | P8, | P4, | P3. |
| **NEXT ROW:** | K4, | K2, | K10, | K2, | K4. |

Break off coral yarn and work using black yarn only.
**Next row:** purl.
**Next row:** K1, (ssK, K1, K2tog) four times, K1 (14 sts).
**Next row:** purl.
**Next row:** K1, (ssK, K2tog) three times, K1 (8 sts).
Thread yarn through remaining sts, leaving a length of yarn for sewing up.

|  | LIGHT GREY | BLACK |
|---|---|---|
| **NEXT ROW:** | (P1, K1) five times, | P1, K1. |

|  | BLACK | LIGHT GREY |
|---|---|---|
| **NEXT ROW:** | (P1, K1) twice, | (P1, K1) four times. |

|  | LIGHT GREY | BLACK |
|---|---|---|
| **NEXT ROW:** | (P1, K1) three times, | (P1, K1) three times. |

## WING (MAKE TWO)

Using light grey yarn, cast on 5 sts and work as follows:
**Next row:** (P1, K1) twice, P1.
**Next row:** Kfb, P1, K1, Pfb, K1 (7 sts).
**Next row:** (P1, K2) twice, P1.
**Next row:** (K1, Pfb, P1) twice, Kfb (10 sts).
**Next row:** Kfb, (P1, K1) four times, Pfb (12 sts).

Break off light grey yarn and work using black yarn only.

**Next row:** (P1, K1) six times.

| | BLACK | CREAM |
|---|---|---|
| **NEXT ROW:** | (P1, K1) three times, P1, | (K1, P1) twice, K1. |
| | CREAM | BLACK |
| **NEXT ROW:** | (P1, K1) three times, P1, | (K1, P1) twice, K1. |

Break off cream yarn and continue using black yarn only.

**Next row:** (P1, K1) six times.
Repeat last row once more.
**Next row:** K2tog, (P1, K1) four times, K2tog (10 sts).
**Next row:** K2tog, (K1, P1) four times (9 sts).
**Next row:** K2tog, (K1, P1) twice, K1, K2tog (7 sts).
**Next row:** K2tog, (K1, P1) twice, K1 (6 sts).
**Next row:** K2tog, P1, K1, K2tog (4 sts).
**Next row:** K2tog, K1, P1 (3 sts).
**Next row:** K1, P1 K1.
Cast off, threading yarn through remaining stitch to fasten.

## TAIL

Using light grey yarn, cast on 7 sts and work as follows:
Starting with a knit row, work 4 rows in SS.
Change to black yarn.
**Next row:** K1, ssK, K1, K2tog, K1 (5 sts).
Starting with a purl row, work 3 rows in SS.
**Next row:** K1, CDD, K1 (3 sts).
Starting with a purl row, work 3 rows in SS.
Purl 2 rows (forms a fold line).
Starting with a knit row, work 4 rows in SS.
**Next row:** (K1, M1) twice, K1 (5 sts).
**Next row:** purl.
**Next row:** K2, sl1, K2.
**Next row:** purl.
Repeat last 2 rows once more.
Cast off, leaving a length of yarn for sewing up.

## FOOT AND LEG (MAKE TWO)

Using dark grey yarn and DPN, cast on 4 sts and work as follows:
**Next row:** cast off 3 sts (1 st).
**\*Next row:** cast on 3 sts (4 sts).
**Next row:** cast off 3 sts (1 st)\*.
Work from \* to \* once more to make three toes, leaving 1 st.
With RS facing, pick up and knit 2 more stitches across the top of the toes (3 sts).
Work 5 rows using the i-cord technique (see page 12).
Thread yarn through remaining sts, leaving a length of yarn for sewing up.

## BEAK

Using dark grey yarn and 3mm (US 2 or 3, UK 11) needles, cast on 5 sts and work as follows:
**Next row:** K2, sl1, K2.
**Next row:** purl.
**Next row:** SsK, K1, K2tog (3 sts).
Thread yarn through remaining sts, leaving a length of yarn for sewing up.

## MAKING UP

Refer to page 21 for general making up instructions.

Taking the body and starting at the cast-off edge (top of the head), sew the seam along the shaped edge, stopping when you reach the cast-off stitches at the back of the head. Place some toy filling inside the head – this will enable you to see exactly how the eyes look before you secure them. Taking the beak, sew the side seam and pin in place, using the photographs for guidance.

Thread the eyes through the knitting, using the photographs for guidance. When you are happy with their position, remove the toy filling and the beak and push the backs onto the safety eyes to secure them. Re-stuff the head with toy filling. Replace the beak and sew firmly in place.

Continue sewing the seam along the back of the bird until you reach the cast-on edge, stuffing with Toy filling as you go. Thread the yarn through the cast-on stitches, gather and secure.

Taking the wings, sew all the ends of yarn into what will be the wrong side. Pin the wings in place on either side of the back centre seam, using the

photographs for guidance. Sew each wing in place along the front edge and for approximately 2cm (¾in) along the top edge.

Taking the tail, pin in place at the back of the body and sew the cast-on edge to the back of the bird. Fold the tail in half at the purled fold line and sew each side seam using matching yarn. Sew the cast-off edge to the bird, using the photographs for guidance.

With the 'toes' at the front and using the photographs for guidance, pin the legs in place either side of the gathered cast-on edge. Sew firmly in place.

# LONG-TAILED TIT

## MATERIALS

→ **DK (light worsted/8-ply) yarn:**
   20m (22yd) in cream
   10m (11yd) in black
   10m (11yd) in pale pink
   1m (1yd) in light grey
→ Two 5mm (¼in) black safety eyes
→ Toy filling

## NEEDLES AND NOTIONS

→ 3mm (US 2 or 3, UK 11) knitting needles
→ 2.5mm (US 1 or 2, UK 12 or 13) knitting needles
→ Darning needle
→ Sharp scissors
→ Pins

## TENSION

→ 7 sts measured over 2.5cm (1in) and worked in SS using 3mm (US 2 or 3, UK 11) needles

## FINISHED SIZE

→ 7cm (2¾in) from top of head to feet

## Instructions

### BODY AND HEAD

Using pale pink yarn, cast on 14 sts and purl 1 row.
Work increase rows as follows (the first row is written out in full to enable you to see the pattern of the increases):
**Next row (RS):** K1, Kfb, K1, Kfb, Kfb, K1, Kfb, Kfb, K1, Kfb, Kfb, K1, Kfb, K1 (22 sts).
**Next row:** purl.
**Next row:** K1, (Kfb, K3, Kfb) to last st, K1 (30 sts).
**Next row:** purl.
**Next row:** K1, M1, K13, M1, K2, M1, K13, M1, K1 (34 sts).
Starting with a purl row, work 3 rows in SS.
Join in cream yarn and work as follows:
**Next row:** (K1 using pale pink yarn, K1 using cream yarn), repeat to the end of the row.
Break off pale pink yarn and continue in cream yarn only.
Starting with a purl row, work 3 rows in SS.

Join in black yarn and continue as follows:

| | BLACK | CREAM | BLACK |
|---|---|---|---|
| **NEXT ROW:** | K10, | K6, M1, K2, M1, K6, | K10 (36 sts). |
| **NEXT ROW:** | P11, | P14, | P11. |
| **NEXT ROW:** | Cast off 6 sts, K4, | K14, | K11 (30 sts). |
| **NEXT ROW:** | Cast off 6 sts, P4, | P14, | P5 (24 sts). |
| **NEXT ROW:** | Cast off 3 sts, K2, | K12, | K6 (21 sts). |
| **NEXT ROW:** | Cast off 3 sts, P2 | P12, | P3 (18 sts). |

Carrying the cream yarn across the row, work as follows:

| | CREAM | BLACK | CREAM | BLACK | CREAM |
|---|---|---|---|---|---|
| **NEXT ROW:** | K2, | K6, | K2, | K6, | K2. |
| **NEXT ROW:** | P3, | P4, | P4, | P4, | P3. |

## WING (MAKE TWO)

Using black yarn, cast on 5 sts and work as follows:
**Next row:** (K1, P1) twice, K1.
**Next row:** Pfb, K1, P1, Kfb, P1 (7 sts).
**Next row:** (K1, P2) twice, K1.
**Next row:** (P1, Kfb, K1) twice, Pfb (10 sts).
**Next row:** (P1, K1) five times.
Change to pale pink yarn.
**Next row:** (P1, K1) five times.
**Next row:** (P1, K1) three times, w&t.
**Next row:** (P1, K1) three times.
**Next row:** (P1, K1) five times.
Change to cream yarn.
**Next row:** (P1, K1) five times.
Repeat last row once more.
Change to black yarn.
**Next row:** (P1, K1) five times.
**Next row:** cast off 2 sts, (K1, P1) twice, K1, P2tog (7 sts).
**Next row:** (K1, P1) three times, K1.
**Next row:** cast off 2 sts, (K1, P1) twice (5 sts).
**Next row:** (K1, P1) twice, K1.
**Next row:** cast off 2 sts, K1, P1 (3 sts).
**Next row:** K1, P1, K1.
**Next row:** cast off 1 st, P1.
**Next row:** K1, P1.
**Next row:** K2tog, threading yarn through remaining st to fasten.

## TAIL

Using 2.5mm (US 1 or 2, UK 12 or 13) needles and black yarn, cast on 5 sts. Starting with a knit row, work 22 rows in SS.
**Next row:** K1, CDD, K1 (3 sts).
Starting with a purl row, work 5 rows in SS.
Thread yarn through remaining sts to fasten.

## BEAK

Using dark grey yarn and 2.5mm (US 1 or 2, UK 12 or 13) needles, cast on 4 sts and purl 1 row.
**Next row:** ssK, K2tog (2 sts).
**Next row:** P2tog, threading yarn through remaining st to fasten.

## MAKING UP

Refer to page 21 for general making up instructions.
   Taking the body and starting at the cast-off edge (top of the head), sew the seam, stopping when you reach the cast-off stitches at the back of the head. Place some toy filling inside the head – this will enable you to see exactly how the eyes look before you secure them. Taking the beak, sew the side seam and pin in place, approximately level with the cast-off stitches along the back of the bird.
   Thread the eyes through the knitting, using the photographs for guidance. Remove the toy filling and beak and push the backs onto the safety eyes to secure them. Re-stuff the head with toy filling. Replace the beak and sew firmly in place.
   Continue sewing the seam along the back of the bird until you reach the cast-on edge, stuffing with toy filling as you go. Thread the yarn through the cast-on stitches, gather and secure.
   Taking the wings, pin them in place on either side of the back centre seam using the photographs for guidance. Sew each wing in place along the front edge and for approximately 2cm (¾in) along the top edge.
   Taking the tail, pin in place at the back of the body, so that the tail sticks out behind the bird. Sew firmly in place. Using light grey yarn and straight stitches, embroider the two feet either side of the centre stitches at the base of the bird. See the photograph of the crossbill's feet on page 117 for guidance.

# PIGEON

## Instructions

### BODY AND HEAD

Using mid grey yarn, cast on 14 sts and purl 1 row. Work increase rows as follows (the first row is written out in full to enable you to see the pattern of the increases):

**Next row (RS):** K1, Kfb, K1, Kfb, Kfb, K1, Kfb, Kfb, K1, Kfb, Kfb, K1, Kfb, K1 (22 sts).

**Next row:** purl.

**Next row:** K1, (Kfb, K3, Kfb) to last st, K1 (30 sts).

**Next row:** purl.

**Next row:** K1, (Kfb, K5, Kfb) to last st, K1 (38 sts).

**Next row:** purl.

**Next row:** K1, (Kfb, K7, Kfb) to last st, K1 (46 sts).

**Next row:** purl.

**Next row:** K1, M1, K21, M1, K2, M1, K21, M1, K1 (50 sts).

**Next row:** purl.

**Next row:** K1, M1, K to last st, M1, K1 (52 sts).

**Next row:** purl.

## MATERIALS

→ **DK (light worsted/8-ply) yarn:**
   20m (22yd) in mid grey
   10m (11yd) in light grey
   3m (3¼yd) in dark grey
   2m (2yd) in green
   2m (2yd) in lilac
   1m (1yd) in cream
   1m (1yd) in salmon pink
→ 10m (11yd) rainbow metallic sewing thread
→ Two 5mm (¼in) black safety eyes
→ Two 2cm (¾in) squares of white felt
→ Toy filling

## NEEDLES AND NOTIONS

→ 3mm (US 2 or 3, UK 11) knitting needles and DPN
→ Darning needle
→ Sharp scissors
→ Pins

## TENSION

→ 7 sts measured over 2.5cm (1in) and worked in SS using 3mm (US 2 or 3, UK 11) needles

## FINISHED SIZE

→ 14cm (5½in) from beak to tail

| | MID GREY | MID GREY AND METALLIC SEWING THREAD | | | MID GREY |
|---|---|---|---|---|---|
| NEXT ROW: | K1, M1, K23, | K1, M1, K2, M1, K1, | | | K23, M1, K1 (56 sts). |
| NEXT ROW: | P24, | P8, | | | P24. |
| NEXT ROW: | K23, | K10, | | | K23. |
| NEXT ROW: | P22, | P12, | | | P22. |
| NEXT ROW: | cast off 5 sts, K15, | K4, ssK, K2, K2tog, K4, | | | K21 (49 sts). |
| NEXT ROW: | cast off 5 sts, P14, | P14, | | | P15 (44 sts). |
| NEXT ROW: | cast off 8 sts, K5, | K5, ssK, K2, K2tog, K5, | | | K14 (34 sts). |
| NEXT ROW: | cast off 8 sts, P4, | P16, | | | P5 (26 sts). |

Continue using mid grey yarn and metallic thread held together.
**Next row:** K1, ssK, K7, ssK, K2, K2tog, K7, K2tog, K1 (22 sts).
Work the rest of the head holding the specified colour of DK yarn *and* a strand of metallic thread together throughout. Break off mid grey yarn and continue as follows, joining in new colours as specified.

| | GREEN | LILAC | GREEN |
|---|---|---|---|
| NEXT ROW: | P6, | P10, | P6. |
| NEXT ROW: | K7, | K8, | K7. |
| NEXT ROW: | P8, | P6, | P8. |
| NEXT ROW: | K9, | K4, | K9. |
| NEXT ROW: | P10, | P2, | P10. |

Break off lilac yarn.
**Next row:** (K1 using green yarn, K1 using mid grey yarn) to end.
Break off green yarn and continue using mid grey yarn.
**Next row:** purl.
**Next row:** K9, ssK, K2tog, K9 (20 sts).
**Next row:** P9, M1, P2, M1, P9 (22 sts).
Starting with a knit row, work 4 rows in SS.
**Next row:** K1, (ssK, K1, K2tog) four times, K1 (14 sts).
**Next row:** purl.
**Next row:** K1, (ssK, K2tog) three times, K1 (8 sts).
Thread yarn through remaining sts, leaving a length of yarn for sewing up.

## WING (MAKE TWO)

Using light grey yarn, cast on 7 sts and work as follows:
**Next row:** Kfb, (P1, K1) twice, P1, Kfb (9 sts).
**Next row:** (K1, P1), four times, K1.
**Next row:** Kfb, (K1, P1) three times, K1, Pfb (11 sts).
**Next row:** Kfb, (K1, P1) four times, K1, Pfb (13 sts).
**Next row:** (P1, K1) six times, P1.
**Next row:** Pfb, (P1, K1) five times, P1, Kfb (15 sts).
**Next row:** (K1, P1) seven times, K1.
**Next row:** (P1, K1) seven times, P1.
Repeat last 2 rows once more.

Change to dark grey yarn.
**Next row:** (K1, P1) seven times, K1.
**Next row:** (P1, K1) seven times, P1.
**Next row:** K2tog, (K1, P1) six times, K1 (14 sts).
Change to light grey yarn.
**Next row:** (P1, K1) six times, K2tog (13 sts).
**Next row:** K2tog, (K1, P1) five times, K1 (12 sts).
**Next row:** (P1, K1) five times, K2tog (11 sts).
**Next row:** K2tog, (K1, P1) four times, K1 (10 sts).
Change to dark grey yarn, without breaking off the light grey yarn.
**Next row:** (P1, K1) four times, K2tog (9 sts).
**Next row:** K2tog, (K1, P1) three times, K1 (8 sts).
Change to light grey yarn.
**Next row:** (P1, K1) three times, K2tog (7 sts).
**Next row:** K2tog, (K1, P1) twice, K1 (6 sts).
**Next row:** (P1, K1) twice, K2tog (5 sts).
**Next row:** K2tog, K1, P1, K1 (4 sts).
**Next row:** P1, K1, K2tog (3 sts).
**Next row:** K2tog, K1 (2 sts).
Thread yarn through remaining sts to fasten.

## TAIL

Using mid grey yarn, cast on 7 sts and work as follows:
**Next row:** (P1, K2) twice, P1.
**Next row:** (K1, P2) twice, K1.
Repeat last 2 rows twice more.
**Next row:** P1, ssK, P1, K2tog, P1 (5 sts).
**Next row:** (K1, P1) twice, K1.
**Next row:** (P1, K1) twice, P1.
Repeat last 2 rows once more.
**Next row:** (K1, P1) twice, K1.
Change to dark grey yarn.
**Next row:** (P1, K1) twice, P1.
**Next row:** (K1, P1) twice, K1.
**Next row:** K2tog, P1, K2tog (3 sts).
**Next row:** P1, K1, P1.
**Next row:** K1, P1, K1.
Cast off.

## FOOT AND LEG (MAKE TWO)

Using salmon pink yarn and DPN, cast on 4 sts and work as follows:
**Next row:** cast off 3 sts (1 st).
***Next row:** cast on 3 sts (4 sts).
**Next row:** cast off 3 sts (1 st)*.
Work from * to * once more to make three toes, leaving 1 st.
With RS facing, pick up and knit 2 more stitches across the top of the toes (3 sts).
Work 3 rows using the i-cord technique (see page 12).
Thread yarn through remaining sts, leaving a length of yarn for sewing up.

## BEAK

Using cream yarn and 3mm (US 2 or 3, UK 11) needles, cast on 3 sts and purl 1 row.
Break off cream yarn.
Using light grey yarn, cast on 1 st, knit across 3 sts on held needle, turn work (4 sts).
**Next row:** cast on 1 st, P to end of row (5 sts).
**Next row:** K2, sl1, K2.
**Next row:** purl.
**Next row:** K1, CDD, K1 (3 sts).
Thread yarn through remaining sts, leaving a length of yarn for sewing up.

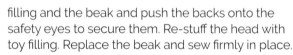

## MAKING UP

First, follow the instructions on page 20 for mounting the safety eyes onto the felt backing and refer to page 21 for general making up instructions.

Taking the body and starting at the cast-off edge (top of the head), sew the seam along the shaped edge, stopping when you reach the cast-off stitches at the back of the head. Place some toy filling inside the head – this will enable you to see exactly how the eyes look before you secure them.

Taking the beak, sew the side seam and pin in place using the photographs for guidance.

Taking a safety eye, cut a 1cm (½in) square of white felt. Fold in half and make a small cut in the centre with sharp scissors, just large enough for the back of the safety eye to thread through. Thread the eye through the hole and trim the felt to leave a 1–2mm (¹/₁₆in) border around the outside of the eye. Repeat for the second eye.

Thread the safety eyes through the knitting. When you are happy with their position, remove the toy filling and the beak and push the backs onto the safety eyes to secure them. Re-stuff the head with toy filling. Replace the beak and sew firmly in place.

Continue sewing the seam along the back of the bird, using matching yarn, until you reach the cast-on edge, stuffing with toy filling as you go. Thread the yarn through the cast-on stitches, gather and secure.

Taking the wings, pin them in place on either side of the back centre seam using the photograph for guidance. Sew each wing in place around the top edges.

Taking the tail piece and using the photograph for guidance, place the cast-on edge of the tail on the body, stretching it out slightly across the tail. Sew the tail onto the body.

With the 'toes' at the front, and using the photographs for guidance, pin the legs in place, either side of the gathered, cast-on edge, using the photographs for guidance. Sew firmly in place.

# SPARROW

## MATERIALS

→ **DK (light worsted/8-ply) yarn:**
   20m (22yd) in light grey
   10m (11yd) in light brown
   10m (11yd) in dark brown
   10m (11yd) in cream
   10m (11yd) in black
   10m (11yd) in dark grey
→ Two 5mm (¼in) black safety eyes
→ Toy filling

## NEEDLES AND NOTIONS

→ 3mm (US 2 or 3, UK 11) knitting
   needles and DPN
→ 2.5mm (US 1 or 2, UK 12 or 13)
   knitting needles
→ Darning needle
→ Sharp scissors
→ Pins

## TENSION

→ 7 sts measured over 2.5cm (1in) and
   worked in SS using 3mm (US 2 or 3,
   UK 11) needles

## FINISHED SIZE

→ 11cm (4¼in) from beak to tail

## Instructions

### BODY AND HEAD

Using light grey yarn, cast on 14 sts and purl 1 row.
Work increase rows as follows (the first row is written out in full to enable you to see the pattern of the increases):
**Next row:** K1, Kfb, K1, Kfb, Kfb, K1, Kfb, Kfb, K1, Kfb, Kfb, K1, Kfb, K1 (22 sts).
**Next row:** purl.
**Next row:** K1, (Kfb, K3, Kfb) to last st, K1 (30 sts).
**Next row:** purl.
**Next row:** K1, (Kfb, K5, Kfb) to last st, K1 (38 sts).
**Next row:** purl.
**Next row:** K1, (Kfb, K7, Kfb) to last st, K1 (46 sts).
Starting with a purl row, work 5 rows in SS.

Join in black yarn and work as follows using the Intarsia technique (see page 13):

| | LIGHT GREY | BLACK | LIGHT GREY |
|---|---|---|---|
| **NEXT ROW:** | K21, | K4, | K21. |
| **NEXT ROW:** | P20, | P6, | P20. |
| **NEXT ROW:** | K20, | K6, | K20. |
| **NEXT ROW:** | P21, | P4, | P21. |

Join in dark brown yarn at each end of the row and work as follows:

| | DARK BROWN | LIGHT GREY | BLACK | LIGHT GREY | DARK BROWN |
|---|---|---|---|---|---|
| **NEXT ROW:** | K12, | K9, | K4, | K9, | K12. |
| **NEXT ROW:** | P13, | P9, | P2, | P9, | P13. |

Without breaking off other yarns, join in cream yarn and work as follows:

| | DARK BROWN | CREAM | BLACK | CREAM | DARK BROWN |
|---|---|---|---|---|---|
| **NEXT ROW:** | cast off 10 sts, K3, | K8, | K2, | K8, | K14 (36 sts). |
| **NEXT ROW:** | cast off 10 sts, P3, | P8, | P2, | P8, | P4 (26 sts). |

Break off cream yarn and work as follows:

| | DARK BROWN | LIGHT GREY | BLACK | LIGHT GREY | DARK BROWN |
|---|---|---|---|---|---|
| **NEXT ROW:** | K1, ssK, K1, | K8, | K2, | K8, | K1, K2tog, K1 (24 sts). |
| **NEXT ROW:** | P1, P2tog, | P8, | P2, | P8, | P2togtbl, P1 (22 sts). |
| **NEXT ROW:** | K2, | K8, | K2, | K8, | K2. |
| **NEXT ROW:** | P3, | P6, | P4, | P6, | P3. |

Without breaking off light grey yarn, work as follows:

|  | DARK BROWN | BLACK | DARK BROWN |
|---|---|---|---|
| **NEXT ROW:** | K7, | K8, | K7. |
| **NEXT ROW:** | P7, | P8, | P7. |

Break off brown and black yarns and continue using light grey yarn only.
**Next row:** knit.
**Next row:** P1, (P2tog, P1, P2togtbl) four times, P1 (14 sts).
**Next row:** K1, (ssK, K2tog) three times, K1 (6 sts).
Thread yarn through remaining sts, leaving a length of yarn for sewing up.

## WING (MAKE TWO)

Using dark brown yarn, cast on 5 sts and work as follows:
**Next row:** (P1, K1) twice, P1.
**Next row:** Kfb, P1, K1, Pfb, K1 (7 sts).
**Next row:** (P1, K2) twice, P1.
**Next row:** (K1, Pfb, P1) twice, Kfb (10 sts).
**Next row:** Kfb, (P1, K1) four times, Pfb (12 sts).
**Next row:** (P1, K1) six times.
Repeat last row once more.
Break off dark brown yarn, change to cream yarn and work as follows:
**Next row:** (P1, K1) six times.
Repeat last row once more.

Break off cream yarn, change to light brown yarn and work as follows:
**Next row:** (P1, K1) six times.
Repeat last row three more times.
**Next row:** cast off 2 sts, (K1, P1) four times, K1 (10 sts).
**Next row:** (P1, K1) five times.
**Next row:** cast off 2 sts, (K1, P1) twice, K1, P2tog (7 sts).
**Next row:** (K1, P1) three times, K1.
**Next row:** cast off 2 sts, K1, P1, K2tog (4 sts).
**Next row:** (P1, K1) twice.
**Next row:** cast off 2 sts, K1 (2 sts).
**Next row:** K2tog, threading yarn through remaining stitch to fasten.

## TAIL

Using dark brown yarn, cast on 5 sts. Starting with a knit row, work 2 rows in SS.

**Next row:** K2, sl1, K2.

**Next row:** purl.

Repeat last 2 rows six more times.

Cast off.

## FOOT AND LEG (MAKE TWO)

Using dark grey yarn and DPN, cast on 4 sts and work as follows:

**Next row:** cast off 3 sts (1 st).

**\*Next row:** cast on 3 sts (4 sts).

**Next row:** cast off 3 sts (1 st)\*.

Work from \* to \* once more to make three toes, leaving 1 st.

With RS facing, pick up and knit 2 more stitches across the top of the toes (3 sts).

Work 5 rows in SS using the i-cord technique (see page 12).

Thread yarn through remaining sts, leaving a length of yarn for sewing up.

## BEAK

Using dark grey yarn and 3mm (US 2 or 3, UK 11) needles, cast on 4 sts.

Starting with a knit row, work 2 rows in SS.

**Next row:** ssK, K2tog (2 sts).

**Next row:** P2tog, threading yarn through remaining st to fasten and leaving a length of yarn for sewing up.

## MAKING UP

Refer to page 21 for general making up instructions.

Taking the body and starting at the cast-off edge (top of the head), sew the seam, stopping when you reach the cast-off stitches at the back of the head. Place some toy filling inside the head – this will enable you to see exactly how the eyes look before you secure them. Taking the beak, sew the side seam and pin in place, approximately level with the cast-off stitches along the back of the bird.

Thread the eyes through the knitting, using the photographs for guidance. Remove the toy filling and beak and push the backs onto the safety eyes to secure them. Re-stuff the head with toy filling. Replace the beak and sew firmly in place.

Continue sewing the seam along the back of the bird until you reach the cast-on edge, stuffing with toy filling as you go. Thread the yarn through the cast-on stitches, gather and secure.

Pin the wings in place on either side of the back centre seam using the photographs for guidance. Sew each wing in place along the front edge and for approximately 2cm (¾in) along the top edge.

Pin the tail in place at the back of the body, so that it sticks out behind the bird. Sew firmly in place.

With the 'toes' at the front and, using the photographs for guidance, pin the legs in place either side of the gathered cast-off edge. Sew firmly in place.

# STARLING

## Instructions

### BODY AND HEAD

Using black yarn and metallic sewing thread held together, cast on 14 sts and purl 1 row.

Work increase rows as follows (the first row is written out in full to enable you to see the pattern of the increases):

**Next row (RS):** K1, Kfb, K1, Kfb, Kfb, K1, Kfb, Kfb, K1, Kfb, Kfb, K1, Kfb, K1 (22 sts).

**Next row:** purl.

**Next row:** K1, (Kfb, K3, Kfb) to last st, K1 (30 sts).

**Next row:** purl.

**Next row:** K1, (Kfb, K5, Kfb) to last st, K1 (38 sts).

**Next row:** purl.

**Next row:** K1, (Kfb, K7, Kfb) to last st, K1 (46 sts).

**Next row:** purl.

**Next row:** K1, M1, K21, M1, K2, M1, K21, M1, K1 (50 sts).

Starting with a purl row, work 5 rows in SS.

Continue in SS, cast off 4 sts at the beginning of the next 2 rows (42 sts).

**Next row:** cast off 8 sts, K23, w&t.

**Next row:** P22, w&t.

**Next row:** K to end of row (34 sts).

**Next row:** cast off 8 sts, P to end of row (26 sts).

**Next row:** K1, ssK, K8, K2tog, ssK, K8, K2tog, K1 (22 sts).

**Next row:** P1, P2tog, P to last 3 sts, P2togtbl, P1 (20 sts).

**Next row:** K9, M1, K2, M1, K9 (22 sts).

Starting with a purl row, work 5 rows in SS.

**Next row:** K1, (ssK, K1, K2tog) four times, K1 (14 sts).

**Next row:** purl.

**Next row:** K1, (ssK, K2tog) three times, K1 (8 sts).

Thread yarn through remaining sts, leaving a length of yarn for sewing up.

### WING (MAKE TWO)

Using black yarn and metallic sewing thread held together, cast on 5 sts and work as follows:

**Next row:** (P1, K1) twice, P1.

**Next row:** Kfb, P1, K1, Pfb, K1 (7 sts).

**Next row:** (P1, K2) twice, P1.

**Next row:** (K1, Pfb, P1) twice, Kfb (10 sts).

**Next row:** Kfb, (P1, K1) four times, Pfb (12 sts).

**Next row:** (P1, K1) six times.

## MATERIALS

→ **DK (light worsted/8-ply) yarn:**
  30m (33yd) in black
  1m (1yd) in yellow
  1m (1yd) in light brown
→ 30m (33yd) metallic rainbow sewing thread
→ Two 5mm (¼in) black safety eyes
→ Toy filling

## NEEDLES AND NOTIONS

→ 3mm (US 2 or 3, UK 11) knitting needles and DPN
→ Darning needle
→ Sharp scissors
→ Pins

## TENSION

→ 7 sts measured over 2.5cm (1in) and worked in SS using 3mm (US 2 or 3, UK 11) needles

## FINISHED SIZE

→ 14cm (5½in) from beak to tail

Repeat last row six more times.
**Next row:** K2tog, (P1, K1) five times (11 sts).
**Next row:** (P1, K1) five times, P1.
**Next row:** K2tog, (K1, P1) four times, K1 (10 sts).
**Next row:** (P1, K1) five times.
**Next row:** K2tog, (P1, K1) four times (9 sts).
**Next row:** (P1, K1) four times, P1.
**Next row:** K2tog, (K1, P1) three times, K1 (8 sts).
**Next row:** K2tog, (P1, K1) three times (7 sts).
**Next row:** K2tog, P1, K1, P1, K2tog (5 sts).
**Next row:** P1, K1, P1, K2tog (4 sts).
**Next row:** K2tog, P1, K1 (3 sts).
**Next row:** P1, K1, P1.
**Next row:** K1, P1, K1.
**Next row:** P1, K1, P1.
**Next row:** CDD (1 st).
Thread yarn through the remaining st to fasten.

## TAIL

Using black yarn and metallic sewing thread held together, cast on 7 sts and work as follows:
**Next row:** (P1, K2) twice, P1.
**Next row:** (K1, P2) twice, K1.
Repeat last 2 rows twice more.
**Next row:** P1, ssK, P1, K2tog, P1 (5 sts).
**Next row:** (K1, P1) twice, K1.
**Next row:** (P1, K1) twice, P1.
Repeat last 2 rows twice more.
**Next row:** (K1, P1) twice, K1.
**Next row:** K2tog, P1, K2tog (3 sts).
**Next row:** P1, K1, P1.
**Next row:** K1, P1, K1.
Cast off.

## FOOT AND LEG (MAKE TWO)

Using light brown yarn and DPN, cast on 4 sts and work as follows:
**Next row:** cast off 3 sts (1 st).
\*\*Next row:** cast on 3 sts (4 sts).
**Next row:** cast off 3 sts (1 st)\*.
Work from \* to \* once more to make three toes, leaving 1 st.
With RS facing, pick up and knit 2 more stitches across the top of the toes (3 sts).
Work 3 rows using the i-cord technique (see page 12).
Thread yarn through remaining sts, leaving a length of yarn for sewing up.

## BEAK

Using yellow yarn and 3mm (US 2 or 3, UK 11) needles, cast on 5 sts and work as follows:
Next row: K2, sl1, K2.
**Next row:** purl.
Repeat last 2 rows once more.
**Next row:** SsK, sl1, K2tog (3 sts).
**Next row:** purl.
**Next row:** CDD (1 st).
Thread yarn through remaining st, leaving a length of yarn for sewing up.

## MAKING UP

Refer to page 21 for general making up instructions. Taking the body and starting at the cast-off edge (top of the head), sew the seam along the shaped edge, stopping when you reach the cast-off stitches at the back of the head. Place some toy filling inside the head – this will enable you to see exactly how the eyes look before you secure them.

Taking the beak, sew the side seam and pin in place, using the photograph for guidance.

Thread the safety eyes through the knitting, using the photographs for guidance. When you are happy with their position, remove the toy filling and beak and push the backs onto the safety eyes to secure them. Re-stuff the head with toy filling. Replace the beak and sew firmly in place. Continue sewing the seam along the back of the bird until you reach the cast-on edge, stuffing with toy filling as you go.

Thread the yarn through the cast-on stitches, gather and secure.

Taking the wings, pin them in place on either side of the back centre seam using the photographs for guidance. Sew each wing in place along the front edge and for approximately 2cm (¾in) along the top edge.

With the 'toes' at the front and using the photographs for guidance, pin the legs in place either side of the gathered cast-on edge. Sew firmly in place.

Pin the tail in place so that the cast-off edge is approximately 2cm (¾in) from the back of the body. Sew firmly in place.

# CRESTED TIT

## Instructions

### BODY AND HEAD

Using beige yarn, cast on 14 sts and purl 1 row.
Work increase rows as follows (the first row is written out in full to enable you to see the pattern of the increases):
**Next row (RS):** K1, Kfb, K1, Kfb, Kfb, K1, Kfb, Kfb, K1, Kfb, Kfb, K1, Kfb, K1 (22 sts).
**Next row:** purl.
**Next row:** K1, (Kfb, K3, Kfb) to last st, K1 (30 sts).
**Next row:** purl.
**Next row:** K1, M1, K13, M1, K2, M1, K13, M1, K1 (34 sts).
Starting with a purl row, work 3 rows in SS.
Join in cream yarn and work as follows using the Intarsia technique (see page 13).

| | BEIGE | CREAM | BEIGE |
|---|---|---|---|
| **NEXT ROW:** | K15, | K4, | K15. |
| **NEXT ROW:** | P13, | P8, | P13. |
| **NEXT ROW:** | K12, | K10, | K12. |
| **NEXT ROW:** | P12, | P10, | P12. |

Do not break off cream yarn and join in black yarn, leaving a long tail so that you can use it to work stitches on later rows and continue as follows:

| | BROWN | BEIGE | BLACK | BEIGE | BROWN |
|---|---|---|---|---|---|
| **NEXT ROW:** | K9, | K3, | K10, | K3, | K9. |

### MATERIALS

→ **DK (light worsted/8-ply) yarn:**
   10m (11yd) in beige
   10m (11yd) in cream
   10m (11yd) in black
   10m (11yd) in brown
   1m (1yd) in grey
→ Two 5mm (¼in) black safety eyes
→ Toy filling

### NEEDLES AND NOTIONS

→ 3mm (US 2 or 3, UK 11) knitting needles
→ Spare needle
→ Darning needle
→ Sharp scissors
→ Pins

### TENSION

→ 7 sts measured over 2.5cm (1in) and worked in SS using 3mm (US 2 or 3, UK 11) needles

### FINISHED SIZE

→ 7cm (2¾in) from top of head to feet

Join in cream yarn and continue as follows:

| | BROWN | BEIGE | BLACK | CREAM | BLACK | BEIGE | BROWN |
|---|---|---|---|---|---|---|---|
| **NEXT ROW:** | P9, | P2, | P2, | P8, | P2, | P2, | P9. |

Break off beige yarn and work as follows:

| | BROWN | BLACK | CREAM | BLACK | BROWN |
|---|---|---|---|---|---|
| **NEXT ROW:** | Cast off 6 sts, K3, | K2, | K10, | K2, | K10 (28 sts). |
| **NEXT ROW:** | Cast off 6 sts, P3, | P1, | P12, | P1, | P4 (22 sts). |
| **NEXT ROW:** | Cast off 3 sts, | K1, | K12, | K1, | K4 (19 sts). |
| **NEXT ROW:** | Cast off 3 sts, | P1, | P12, | P1, | P1 (16 sts). |

Break off brown yarn and work as follows:

| | BLACK | CREAM | BLACK |
|---|---|---|---|
| **NEXT ROW:** | K2tog, | K12, | ssK (14 sts). |
| **NEXT ROW:** | P2tog, | P10, | P2togtbl (12 sts). |

Take approximately 1m (1yd) of black yarn and separate out one individual ply of yarn. Hold this strand together with a matching length of cream yarn and work as follows:

**Next row:** K6, turn work.
**Next row:** sl1, P5, turn work.
**Next row:** K1, M1, knit to end.
**Next row:** P6, turn work.
**Next row:** sl1, K4, M1, K1, turn work.
**Next row:** P7.
With WS together, cast off using the three-needle cast-off technique (see page 15).

## WING (MAKE TWO)

Using brown yarn, cast on 5 sts and work as follows:
**Next row:** (K1, P1) twice, K1.
**Next row:** Pfb, K1, P1, Kfb, P1 (7 sts).
**Next row:** (K1, P2) twice, K1.
**Next row:** (P1, Kfb, K1) twice, Pfb (10 sts).
**Next row:** (P1, K1) five times.
Repeat last row twice more.
**Next row:** cast off 2 sts, (K1, P1) twice, K1, P2tog
(7 sts).
**Next row:** (K1, P1) three times, K1.
**Next row:** cast off 2 sts, (K1, P1) twice (5 sts).
**Next row:** (K1, P1) twice, K1.
**Next row:** cast off 2 sts, K1, P1 (3 sts).
**Next row:** K1, P1, K1.
**Next row:** cast off 1 st, P1.
**Next row:** K2tog, threading yarn through
remaining st to fasten.

## TAIL

Using brown yarn, cast on 5 sts.
**Next row:** K2, sl1, K2.
**Next row:** purl.
Repeat last two rows once more.
**Next row:** K1, CDD, K1 (3 sts).
**Next row:** purl.
**Next row:** CDD.
Thread yarn through remaining st and fasten.

## BEAK

Using grey yarn cast on 4 sts and purl 1 row.
**Next row:** ssK, K2tog (2 sts).
**Next row:** P2tog (1 st).
Thread yarn through remaining st to fasten, leaving a
length of yarn for sewing up.

## MAKING UP

Refer to page 21 for general making up instructions.

Taking the body and starting at the cast-off edge
(top of the head), sew the seam, stopping when you
reach the cast-off stitches at the back of the head.
Place some toy filling inside the head – this will
enable you to see exactly how the eyes look before
you secure them. Taking the beak, sew the side
seam and pin in place, approximately level with the
cast-off stitches along the back of the bird.

Thread the eyes through the knitting, using the
photographs for guidance. Remove the toy filling
and beak and push the backs onto the safety eyes

to secure them. Re-stuff the head with toy filling.
Replace the beak and sew firmly in place.

Continue sewing the seam along the back of the
bird until you reach the cast-on edge, stuffing with
toy filling as you go. Thread the yarn through the
cast-on stitches, gather and secure.

Taking the wings, pin them in place on either side
of the back centre seam using the photographs for
guidance. Sew each wing in place along the front
edge and for approximately 2cm (¾in) along the
top edge.

Taking the tail, pin the cast-off edge to the top
of the back of the body, using the photographs for
guidance, and sew in place.

Using grey yarn and straight stitches, embroider a
foot either side of the centre stitches at the base of
the bird. See the photograph of the crossbill's feet
on page 117 for guidance.

# CAPERCAILLIE

## Instructions

### BODY AND HEAD

Using black yarn, cast on 14 sts and purl 1 row.
Work increase rows as follows (the first row is written out in full to enable you to see the pattern of the increases):
**Next row:** K1, Kfb, K1, Kfb, Kfb, K1, Kfb, Kfb, K1, Kfb, Kfb, K1, Kfb, K1 (22 sts).
**Next row:** purl.
**Next row:** K1, (Kfb, K3, Kfb) to last st, K1 (30 sts).
**Next row:** purl.
**Next row:** K1, (Kfb, K5, Kfb) to last st, K1 (38 sts).
**Next row:** purl.
**Next row:** K1, (Kfb, K7, Kfb) to last st, K1 (46 sts).
**Next row:** purl.
Join in dark green yarn and work as follows using the intarsia technique (see page 13).

| | BLACK | DARK GREEN | BLACK |
|---|---|---|---|
| **NEXT ROW:** | K21, | K4, | K21. |
| **NEXT ROW:** | P19, | P8, | P19. |
| **NEXT ROW:** | K17, | K12, | K17. |
| **NEXT ROW:** | P15, | P16, | P15. |
| **NEXT ROW:** | K14, | K18, | K14. |
| **NEXT ROW:** | P14, | P15, w&t. K12, w&t. P15, | P14. |
| **NEXT ROW:** | K4, w&t, purl to the end of the row. K14, | K18, | K14. |
| **NEXT ROW:** | P4, w&t, knit to end of row. P14, | P18, | P14. |
| **NEXT ROW:** | cast off 12 sts, K5, | K10, | K18 (34 sts). |
| **NEXT ROW:** | cast off 12 sts, K5, P2, | P6, | P2, K6 (22 sts). |

## MATERIALS

→ **DK (light worsted/8-ply) yarn:**
  30m (33yd) in black
  10m (11yd) in brown
  10m (11yd) in dark green
  10m (11yd) in white
  1m (1yd) in red
  10m (11yd) in pale yellow
  1m (1yd) in grey
→ Two 5mm (¼in) black safety eyes
→ Toy filling

## NEEDLES AND NOTIONS

→ 3mm (US 2 or 3, UK 11) knitting needles and DPN
→ Darning needle
→ Sharp scissors
→ Pins

## TENSION

→ 7 sts measured over 2.5cm (1in) and worked in SS using 3mm (US 2 or 3, UK 11) needles

## FINISHED SIZE

→ 11cm (4¼in) from beak to tail

Break off dark green yarn and continue using black yarn only and working in reverse SS.
**Next row:** P1, P2tog, P5, K6, P5, P2togtbl, P1 (20 sts).
**Next row:** knit.
**Next row:** P1, P2tog, P to last 3 sts, P2togtbl, P1 (18 sts).
**Next row:** rep last 2 rows twice more (14 sts).
Starting with a purl row, work 2 rows in reverse SS.
**Next row:** P4, P2tog, P2, P2togtbl, P4 (12 sts).
**Next row:** K1, M1, K4, M1, K2, M1, K4, M1, K1 (16 sts).
Starting with a P row, work 3 rows in SS.
**Next row:** K1, ssK, K1, K2tog, K2, ssK, K2, K2tog, K1 (12 sts).
**Next row:** P1, P2tog, P1, P2togtbl, P2tog, P1, P2togtbl, P1 (8 sts).
Thread yarn through remaining sts, leaving a length of yarn for sewing up.

### TAIL FEATHERS (LARGER SECTION)

Using black yarn, cast on 5 sts and work as follows:
**Next row:** (K1, M1) four times, K1 (9 sts).
**Next row:** purl.
Repeat the last 2 rows twice more (33 sts).
**Next row:** K6, M1, (K5, M1) four times, K7 (38 sts).
**Next row:** purl.
**Next row:** (K2, P2) to last 2 sts, K2.
**Next row:** (P2, K2) to last 2 sts, P2.
Repeat the last 2 rows three more times.
Join in white yarn:
**Next row:** (K2, P2) to last 2 sts, K2.
Break off white yarn and continue using black yarn.
**Next row:** (P2, K2) to last 2 sts, P2.
**Next row:** (K2, K2tog, YO) to last 2 sts, K2.
**Next row:** (P2, K2) to last 2 sts, P2.
**Next row:** (K2, P2) to last 2 sts, K2.
Repeat last 2 rows twice more.
**Next row:** (P2, K2tog) to last 2 sts, P2 (29 sts).
**Next row:** (K2, P1) to last 2 sts, K2.
**Next row:** (P2tog, K1) to last 2 sts, P2tog (19 sts).
**Next row:** (K2tog) eight times, K1, K2tog (10 sts).
**Next row:** (P2tog) five times (5 sts).
Thread yarn through remaining sts, gather and fasten.

### TAIL FEATHERS (SMALLER SECTION)

Using white yarn, cast on 7 sts and work 2 rows in SS.
**Next row:** (K1, M1) six times, K1 (13 sts).
**Next row:** purl.
**Next row:** (K2, M1) six times, K1 (19 sts).
**Next row:** purl.
**Next row:** (K1, M1) twice, (K2, M1) six times, (K1, M1) three times, K2 (30 sts).
**Next row:** purl.
**Next row:** (K2, P2) to last 2 sts, K2.
**Next row:** (P2, K2) to last 2 sts, P2.
Repeat the last 2 rows twice more.
Cast off in rib.

### WING (MAKE TWO)

Using brown yarn, cast on 5 sts and purl 1 row.
**Next row:** K1, M1, K to last st, M1, K1 (7 sts).
**Next row:** P1, M1, P to last st, M1, P1 (9 sts).
Starting with a knit row, work 6 rows in SS.
Cast off 1 st at the beginning of the next 6 rows.
Cast off remaining 3 sts.

## FOOT (MAKE TWO)

Using grey yarn and DPN cast on 6 sts.
**Next row:** cast off 4 sts, K1 (2 sts).
**\*Next row:** K2.
**Next row:** cast on 4 sts, cast off 4 sts, K1 (2 sts)\*.
Work from \* to \* once more to make a third toe,
casting off 5 sts on the last row (1 st).
With RS facing, pick up and knit 2 sts across
the top of the toes (3 sts).
Work 3 rows in SS using the i-cord technique
(see page 12). Thread yarn through sts to fasten,
leaving a length of yarn for sewing up.

## EYE PIECE (MAKE TWO)

Using red yarn and 3mm (US 2 or 3, UK 11)
needles, cast on 2 sts.
**Next row:** K1, M1, K1 (3 sts).
**Next row:** purl.
Cast off.

## BEAK

Using pale yellow yarn cast on 5 sts.
**Next row:** K2, sl1, K2.
**Next row:** purl.
**Next row:** K1, CDD, K1 (3 sts).
**Next row:** purl.
**Next row:** CDD (1 st).
Thread yarn through remaining st to fasten, leaving a
length of yarn for sewing up.

## MAKING UP

Refer to page 21 for general making up instructions
   Taking the body and starting at the cast-off edge
(top of the head), sew the seam, stopping when you
reach the cast-off stitches at the back of the head.
Place some toy filling inside the head – this will
enable you to see exactly how the eyes look before
you secure them. Taking the beak, sew the side
seam and pin in place, approximately level with the
cast-off stitches along the back of the bird. Pin the
eye pieces in place.
   Taking one of the eyes, push through one red eye
piece between the two cast-on stitches. Repeat for
the second eye.
   Thread the eyes through the knitting, using the
photographs for guidance. Remove the toy filling
and beak and push the backs onto the safety eyes
to secure them. Re-stuff the head with toy filling.

Replace the beak and sew firmly in place.
   Continue sewing the seam along the back of the
bird until you reach the cast-on edge, stuffing with toy
filling as you go. Thread the yarn through the cast-on
stitches, gather and secure.
   Taking the larger tail section, fold in half with the
eyelet stitches forming the fold line. Pin in place at the
back of the body, using the photograph for guidance
and with the cast-on edge toward the front of the bird.
Stretching each side slightly to form a rounded shape,
sew the cast on edge to the top of the back of the
bird and the cast-off edge to the back of the bird. Sew
the side seams. Taking the smaller tail section, sew
in place behind the main tail section so that the tail
sticks up behind the bird. Sew firmly in place.
   Taking a wing, pin in place using the photographs
for guidance and stretching slightly. Sew in place
along the top, front and bottom edges. Place a small
amount of toy filling inside to add definition. Using
white yarn, embroider a small 'patch' on each wing
using straight stitches and using the photographs for
guidance. Repeat for the second wing.
   With the 'toes' at the front and using the
photographs for guidance, pin the feet in place either
side of the gathered cast-on edge. Sew firmly in place.

# CROSSBILL

## Instructions

### BODY AND HEAD

Using cream yarn cast on 14 sts and purl 1 row.
Work increase rows as follows (the first row is written out in full to enable you to see the pattern of the increases):
**Next row (RS):** K1, Kfb, K1, Kfb, Kfb, K1, Kfb, Kfb, K1, Kfb, Kfb, K1, Kfb, K1 (22 sts).
**Next row:** purl.
**Next row:** K1, (Kfb, K3, Kfb) to last st, K1 (30 sts).
**Next row:** purl.
Join in orange yarn and work as follows using the Intarsia technique (see page 13).

| | CREAM | ORANGE | CREAM |
|---|---|---|---|
| **NEXT ROW:** | K12, | K6, | K12. |
| **NEXT ROW:** | P9, | P12, | P9. |
| **NEXT ROW:** | K5, | K20, | K5. |
| **NEXT ROW:** | P3, | P26, | P3. |

Break off cream yarn and continue using orange yarn only.
Starting with a knit row, work 4 rows in SS.
Cast off 5 sts at beginning of next two rows (20 sts).
Cast off 2 sts at beginning of next row (18 sts).
**Next row:** cast off 2 sts, P4, P2tog, P2, P2togtbl, P5 (14 sts).
**Next row:** K6, M1, K2, M1, K6 (16 sts).
Starting with a purl row, work 3 rows in SS.
**Next row:** K1, ssK, K2, K2tog, K2, ssK, K2, K2tog, K1 (12 sts).
**Next row:** purl.
**Next row:** K1, ssK, K1, K2tog, ssK, K1, K2tog, K1 (8 sts).
Divide the remaining 8 sts evenly between two needles and with RS together, cast off using the three-needle cast-off technique.

## MATERIALS

→ **DK (light worsted/8-ply) yarn:**
  10m (11yd) in brown
  10m (11yd) in orange
  10m (11yd) in cream
  1m (1yd) in grey
→ Two 5mm (¼in) black safety eyes
→ Toy filling

## NEEDLES AND NOTIONS

→ 3mm (US 2 or 3, UK 11) knitting needles
→ Darning needle
→ Sharp scissors
→ Pins

## TENSION

→ 7 sts measured over 2.5cm (1in) and worked in SS using 3mm (US 2 or 3, UK 11) needles

## FINISHED SIZE

→ 117cm (2¾in) from top of head to feet

## WING (MAKE TWO)

Using brown yarn, cast on 5 sts and work as follows:
**Next row:** (K1, P1) twice, K1.
**Next row:** Pfb, K1, P1, Kfb, P1 (7 sts).
**Next row:** (K1, P2) twice, K1.
**Next row:** (P1, Kfb, K1) twice, Pfb (10 sts).
**Next row:** (P1, K1) five times.
**Repeat last** row twice more.
**Next row:** cast off 2 sts, (K1, P1) twice, K1, P2tog
(7 sts).
**Next row:** (K1, P1) three times, K1.
**Next row:** cast off 2 sts, (K1, P1) twice (5 sts).
**Next row:** (K1, P1) twice, K1.
**Next row:** cast off 2 sts, K1, P1 (3 sts).
**Next row:** K1, P1, K1.
**Next row:** cast off 1 st, P1 (2 sts).
**Next row:** K1, P1.
**Next row:** K2tog, threading yarn through
remaining st to fasten.

## TAIL

Using brown yarn, cast on 5 sts.
**Next row:** K2, sl1, K2.
**Next row:** purl.
Repeat the last 2 rows four more times.
Cast off, leaving a length of yarn for sewing the tail
in place.

## BEAK

Using grey yarn, cast on 4 sts and, starting with a knit row, work 2 rows in SS.

**Next row:** K2tog, thread the yarn through resulting st to fasten and break yarn.

Using the cast-on end of yarn, K2tog and fasten off resulting st in the same way.

Sew the small seam, sewing the two cast-off sts lightly in place to give the appearance of a 'crossed' beak.

## MAKING UP

Refer to page 21 for general making up instructions. Taking the body and starting at the cast-off edge (top of the head), sew the seam, stopping when you reach the cast-off stitches at the back of the head. Place some toy filling inside the head – this will enable you to see exactly how the eyes look before you secure them. Taking the beak, sew the side seam and pin in place, approximately level with the cast-off stitches along the back of the bird.

Thread the eyes through the knitting, using the photographs for guidance. Remove the toy filling and beak and push the backs onto the safety eyes to secure them. Re-stuff the head with toy filling. Replace the beak and sew firmly in place.

Continue sewing the seam along the back of the bird until you reach the cast-on edge, stuffing with toy filling as you go. Thread the yarn through the cast-on stitches, gather and secure.

Pin the tail in place at the back of the body, so that it sticks out behind the bird. Sew firmly in place. Using light grey yarn and straight stitches, embroider a foot on either side of the centre stitches at the base of the bird using the photograph (right) for guidance.

# DISPLAY IDEAS

# Hanging nest

If you want to make a cute, knitted hanging nest to display a bird, just follow the pattern here. This nest is felted in the washing machine after knitting, which makes the stitches much less visible and gives it a fluffy texture. You need to use pure wool yarn in order for your nest to felt properly.

## BODY

Cast on 14 sts and purl 1 row.
Work increase rows as follows (the first row is written out in full to enable you to see the pattern of the increases):
**Next row:** K1, Kfb, K1, Kfb, Kfb, K1, Kfb, Kfb, K1, Kfb, Kfb, K1, Kfb, K1 (22 sts).
**Next row:** purl.
**Next row:** K1, (Kfb, K3, Kfb) to last st, K1 (30 sts).
**Next row:** purl.
**Next row:** K1, (Kfb, K5, Kfb) to last st, K1 (38 sts).
**Next row:** purl.
**Next row:** K1, (Kfb, K7, Kfb) to last st, K1 (46 sts).
**Next row:** purl.
**Next row:** K1, (Kfb, K9, Kfb) to last st, K1 (54 sts).
**Next row:** purl.
**Next row:** K1, (Kfb, K11, Kfb) to last st, K1 (62 sts).
**Next row:** purl.
**Next row:** K1, (Kfb, K13, Kfb) to last st, K1 (70 sts).
**Next row:** purl.
Starting with a knit row, work 2 rows in SS.
**Next row:** K32, cast off 6 sts, knit to the end of the row (leaving two groups of 32 sts).
Working only over the first set of 32 sts, work as follows:
**Next row:** purl.
**Next row:** K1, ssK, knit to the end of the row (31 sts).
**Next row:** purl.
Repeat the last 2 rows once more (30 sts).
Starting with a knit row, work 4 rows in SS.
**Next row:** K1, M1, knit to the end of the row (31 sts).
**Next row:** purl.
Repeat the last 2 rows once more (32 sts).
Leave these sts on a spare needle or stitch holder. With WS facing, rejoin the yarn to the remaining 32 sts and work as follows:

MATERIALS
→ 70m (76½yd) of chunky (bulky) pure wool yarn in beige (do not use superwash yarn); I used Icelandic lopi yarn

NEEDLES AND NOTIONS
→ 4.5mm (US 7, UK 7) knitting needles
→ Sharp scissors
→ Spare needle or stitch holder
→ A round balloon

**Next row:** purl.
**Next row:** K to last 3 sts, K2tog, K1 (31 sts).
**Next row:** purl.
Repeat the last 2 rows once more (30 sts).
Starting with a knit row, work 4 rows in SS.
**Next row:** K to last st, M1, K1 (31 sts).
**Next row:** purl.
Repeat the last 2 rows once more (32 sts).
**Next row:** K32, turn work and cast on 6 sts, turn work and knit the 32 sts held on the spare needle or stitch holder to join both pieces (70 sts).
**Next row:** purl.
**Next row:** K1, (ssK, K13, K2tog) to last st, K1 (62 sts).
Starting with a purl row, work 3 rows in SS.
**Next row:** K1, (ssK, K11, K2tog) to last st, K1 (54 sts).
Starting with a purl row, work 3 rows in SS.
**Next row:** K1, (ssK, K9, K2tog) to last st, K1 (46 sts).
Starting with a purl row, work 3 rows in SS.
**Next row:** K1, (ssK, K7, K2tog) to last st, K1 (38 sts).
**Next row:** purl.

**Next row:** K1, (ssK, K5, K2tog) to last st, K1 (30 sts).
**Next row:** purl.
**Next row:** K1, (ssK, K3, K2tog) to last st, K1 (22 sts).
Starting with a purl row, work 3 rows in SS.
**Next row:** K1, (ssK, K1, K2tog) to last st, K1 (14 sts).
**Next row:** purl.
**Next row:** K1, (ssK, K2tog) three times, K1 (8 sts).
**Next row:** purl.
**Next row:** (ssK, K2tog) twice (4 sts).
Starting with a purl row, work 19 rows in SS.
Thread yarn through remaining sts to fasten, leaving a length of yarn for sewing up.

## MAKING UP

Starting at the top, fold the narrow section over and sew to the top of the nest to make a loop. Sew the seam, which will be at the back of the nest, making sure that the seam is not too bulky. Thread the yarn through the cast-on stitches and gather to close. Secure the yarn.

Now place the nest in the washing machine with some washing powder – the heat and agitation will help the yarn to felt. I washed my nest on a 40 degree standard wash. Be brave! If your nest does not shrink enough, repeat the process. After felting, you can try it for size with a bird you have already made to see if it fits. When you are happy with the size, take the nest out of the machine and inflate a balloon inside it to make the round shape. Place it somewhere warm and leave it to dry.

# Felt birdhouse

Trace the nest box pattern pieces from the template page (140-141) and transfer onto card (I used a cereal box). Cut out the pattern pieces and place onto the felt. Using an erasable marker pen, draw around the templates and cut the pieces out. Lightly iron each piece to remove any pen marks.

**1** Using three strands of grey embroidery thread with a knot at one end, hold the base and the back piece of the birdhouse together and, placing the knot in the middle, make a couple of overstitches in the same place to secure.

**2** Then start working blanket stitch along one side.

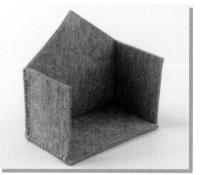

**3** Sew both side pieces to the joined back and base piece, again using blanket stitch.

**4** First, work blanket stitch around the entrance to the house using grey thread. Then embroider flowers on the front of the house using lazy daisy stitch (see page 23) and pink and yellow embroidery thread. If you wish, cut out a pink felt heart and attach it to the top of the house front using blanket stitch and green thread. Then embroider a stem between each flower using green thread and backstitch.

**5** Using grey thread and blanket stitch, join the front of the house to the sides and the base. Then blanket stitch the two roof pieces together along the apex.

**6** Apply a line of glue all round the top edges of the house and place the roof on top, sticking it firmly to the house.

The finished birdhouse.

123

# Felt-covered branches

The branches are made by stretching narrow strips of felt and then wrapping them around the branch. Be careful to start and finish wrapping at the point where you are going to place your decoration, so that you hide any joins.

## YOU WILL NEED:

→ A branch from the garden
→ Brown-grey felt cut into 1–1.5cm (¼–½in) strips
→ Strong all-purpose glue
→ Scissors

**1** Pull the first felt strip to stretch it a little and fray the edges slightly. Place a dot of glue on the end of the strip and fold it over the end of one of the smaller branches (do these first).

**2** Continue wrapping and overlapping slightly as you go.

**3** When you get to the main stem cut the felt, leaving a tab to glue. Place a dot of glue on the felt tab.

**4** Stick the tab round the main stem to secure it.

**5** Once all the small branches are done, you can cover the main stem. Glue the end and, starting at the top (the narrowest end), begin wrapping the felt round the stem.

**6** When you reach the junction with a side stem, place a dot of glue on the felt to stop it slipping and carry on winding it round the stem. Place a dot of glue at each junction to stop the felt slipping.

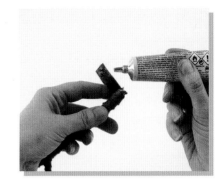

**7** At the end of the stem, place a dot of glue on the felt and the stick and press firmly to secure it. Allow to dry.

The finished branch.

If you wish, you can use your branch horizontally to display your birds.

# Hanging hoops

The hanging hoops are made in the same way as the branches, by stretching narrow strips of felt and then wrapping them around the hoop. Be careful to start and finish wrapping at the point where you are intending to place the decoration, so that you hide any joins.

Flowers and leaves can be sewn in place using matching yarn. The bird is sewn on afterwards. Make sure you sew the feet so it looks as though the bird is sitting on a branch. If you would like to swap your birds, use pins to attach them to the hoop.

**1** Pull the first felt strip to stretch it a little and fray the edges slightly.

**2** Starting where you intend to place your decorations, wrap the felt over two or three times and pull it tightly to secure the loose end.

**3** Continue to wrap, overlapping the felt slightly as you wrap it over the hoop.

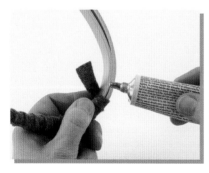

**4** When you come to the end of a felt strip, place a dot of glue on the underside (against the wood) and stick the felt down on the inside of the hoop.

**5** Trim off any excess felt.

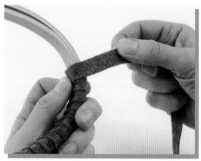

**6** Stretch the next strip of felt and overlap it a few times as you did at the beginning, to secure the loose end, holding it steady with your thumb.

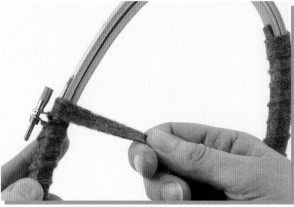

7 Wrap the felt up to the clamp...

8 ...and take it neatly round the other side to continue wrapping.

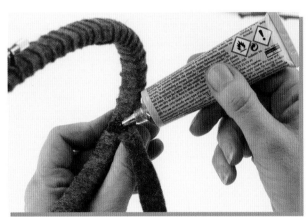

9 Once you meet the other side of the felt, place a dot of glue on the underside and stick it down. Trim off the excess felt and the hoop is done.

The finished hoop. If you pin your bird onto the hoop, you can change it for another bird at any time. If you want it to be more permanent, sew the bird firmly onto the felt.

Seaside hoop

Festive hoop

Autumn hoop

Apple blossom hoop

Clouds hoop

Tropical hoop

# Leaves

Leaves are really easy to make, either by hand sewing or using a sewing machine with free machine embroidery.

## HAND SEWING A LEAF

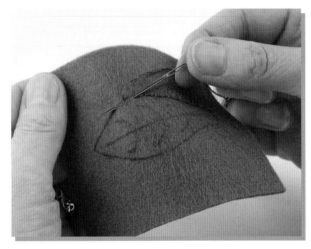

**1** Using an erasable marker pen, trace the leaf outline and veins onto the felt using the template on page 143. Stitch around the outline of the leaf using backstitch.

**2** Work up the centre vein, again using backstitch, and go off to the right or left each time you reach a side vein.

**3** When all the veins are stitched, fasten off securely at the back and iron the felt carefully to remove the pen marks.

**4** Cut out the leaf, leaving a few millimetres (⅛in) between the stitching and your cutting line.

## MACHINE SEWING A LEAF

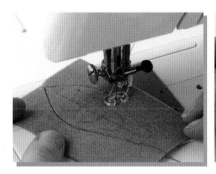 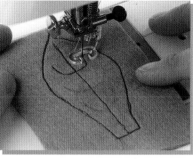 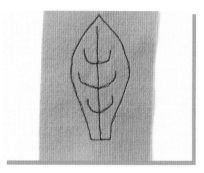

**1** Trace the leaf pattern onto the felt as before. Start stitching around the outline of the leaf, but this time go round the outline twice.

**2** Work up the centre vein to the top, then come back down, but go off to the right or left as you reach each side vein. This ensures that you have a double line of stitching throughout.

**3** Fasten off and iron the felt carefully to remove the pen marks.

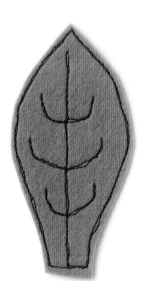 

**4** Cut out the leaf, leaving a few millimetres (⅛in) between the stitching and your cutting line.

Machine stitching produces a different look from hand sewing. Compare the leaves on the right with the hand-sewn one opposite.

# Flowers

I made two flowers to decorate the display hoops. They are easy to make and look very effective.

## APPLE BLOSSOM

**1** Cut out the template pieces in white and yellow felt.

**2** Take the yellow piece of felt and roll it up. Just before you finish, place a dab of glue onto the end.

**3** Stick a pin through the end of the rolled-up felt and leave it to dry.

**4** Now take the white piece of felt and apply a line of blusher all the way down the middle but slightly off centre.

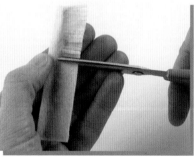

**5** Make narrow snips – about 2-3mm (⅛in) apart – two-thirds of the way down the width of the felt and all the way down the length.

**6** Place a dot of glue near the join on the yellow flower centre.

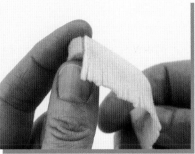

**7** Start attaching the white strip with the blusher facing the inside.

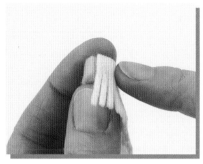

**8** Wrap it round the flower centre, pulling slightly as you go, so that it is fairly tight.

**9** When you reach the end, place a dot of glue on the felt where the end of the strip will sit and stick firmly.

**10** Pin as before and leave it to dry.

**11** When the glue is dry, fan out the petals and the flower is ready to be used.

# TROPICAL FLOWER

**1** Cut out all the felt pieces. Stitch along the dotted lines on the outer pink petals using a sewing machine or needle and thread.

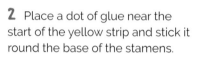

**2** Place a dot of glue near the start of the yellow strip and stick it round the base of the stamens.

**3** Roll it up fairly tightly, place another dot of glue near the end and stick it down.

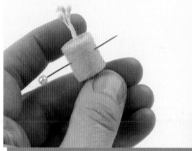

**4** Stick a pin through the rolled-up felt and leave it to dry.

**5** Now take the orange inner petal section and wind it round the flower centre, placing a dab of glue at the beginning and another at the end.

**6** When it's dry, stick on the outer petals one by one, overlapping them slightly, and leave to dry.

**7** Fan out the inner and outer petals to reveal the flower centre.

**8** To make the stem, place the chenille stick lengthwise in the centre of the green felt and pin.

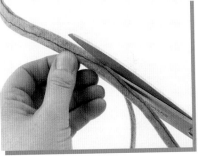

**9** Machine stitch or hand sew the seam and trim off the excess felt.

**10** Place a dot of glue into the flower centre, push the stem into it and pin.

**11** Now cut a piece of green felt long enough to go round the base of the flower. Pin to check the fit.

**12** Unpin the green felt, snip about two-thirds of the way down all around and glue it to the base so it follows the contours of the petals.

**13** Make a leaf as shown on page 130–131 and make a few stitches at the base to curve the leaf.

**14** Attach the leaf by sewing through the base of the leaf and the stem. If you wish, you can attach one or two more leaves at different points on the stem.

# Pebbles

The pebbles are very quick and easy to make and fit nicely onto an embroidery hoop as an embellishment.

YOU WILL NEED:
→ Small amount of light grey and dark grey felt
→ Sewing machine or needle
→ Sewing thread
→ Scissors
→ Pins

**1** Cut out two small or large pebbles in felt using the template on page 142.

**2** Sew the darts on each piece and place right sides together, matching the darts.

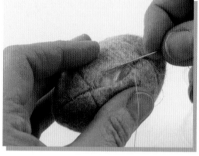

**3** Sew the seam leaving a 5mm (¼in) seam allowance and a turning gap of about 3cm (1¼in).

**4** Turn through, stuff firmly and sew up the gap using ladder stitch. Pull fairly tightly so the stuffing doesn't show through.

**5** The sewn-up pebble.

**6** Cut a thin strip of contrasting felt that goes all the way round one end of the pebble. Stretch it slightly to fray the edges and pin in place.

**7** Sew the strip to the pebble using matching thread and small stitches and fasten off securely.

# Grass clump

I used a grass clump to decorate the seaside hoop (see page 128). They are super-quick to make and look great.

Simply cut the template shape (see page 143) out of green felt. Place a dab of glue at the beginning and roll it up. Just before the end, place another dab of glue on the felt and stick it down. Put a pin through it and leave to dry. It is then ready to use and can either be glued down or sewn into position.

# Mistletoe

This could be used on the festive hoop instead of the holly leaves.

To make the mistletoe, simply draw the shape onto green felt using the template on page 142. Sew around the edge of the shape, about 3mm (⅛in) in from the edge, then cut it out.

## TO MAKE THE BERRIES

Using white yarn and 3mm (US 2 or 3, UK 11) DPN, cast on 1 st.
**Next row:** Kfbf (3 sts).
**Next row:** Kfb, P1, Kfb (5 sts).
Starting with a knit row, work 2 rows in SS.
**Next row:** K2tog, K1, K2tog (3 sts).
**Next row:** sl1, P2tog, psso (1 st).
Thread yarn through remaining st and fasten, leaving a length of yarn for sewing up.

## MAKING UP

Using a darning needle, run your needle around the outside edge of the berry. Place a small ball of toy filling in the middle of the berry and gather. Secure your thread and fasten.

## MATERIALS

→ Small amount of DK (light worsted/8-ply) yarn in white
→ Toy filling
→ Small amount of green felt
→ Sewing thread

## TOOLS

→ 3mm (US 2 or 3, UK 11) DPN
→ Sewing machine or needle
→ Darning needle

To make the holly berries, work the same pattern as for the mistletoe berries using red yarn.

138

# Pine cone

I used pine cones to display the crossbill (see page 115) and they are very effective. You could also attach one to a felt-covered embroidery hoop.

Cast on 40 sts, leaving a long yarn tail.
**Next row:** (Kfb) forty times (80 sts).
**Next row:** K60, w&t.
**Next row:** knit to the end of the row.
**Next row:** K40, w&t.
**Next row:** knit to the end of the row.
Cast off using the picot cast-off technique as follows:
Cast on 2 sts, cast off 3 sts. Repeat to the end of the row.

## MAKING UP

Following the natural curl of the pine cone, twist until you have achieved the shape you need and, using brown yarn, sew the stalk in place at the top, sewing the small seam that will appear at the top of the pine cone. Run your needle and yarn through all the layers of the pine cone to the bottom and back up to secure the shape and layers in place.

## MATERIALS
→ 30m (33yd) of DK (light worsted/8-ply) yarn in brown

## NEEDLES AND NOTIONS
→ 3mm (US 2 or 3, UK 11) knitting needles
→ Darning needle

# Acorn

I used these to decorate the autumn hoop (see page 128) with some oak leaves.

## ACORN

Using yellow yarn, cast on 7 sts and, starting with a knit row, work 6 rows in SS.
Thread yarn through sts and fasten, leaving a length of yarn for sewing up.

## CUP

Using brown yarn, cast on 3 sts and work 5 rows using the i-cord technique (see page 12).
**Next row:** (Kfb twice, K1) (5 sts).
**Next row:** purl.
**Next row:** (Kfb) 4 times, K1 (9 sts).
**Next row:** purl.
**Next row:** knit.
Cast off.

## MAKING UP

Taking the acorn, gather the cast-off edge and sew the side seam. Stuff gently with toy filling. Gather the cast-on edge and secure. Taking the cup, with the WS facing outwards, sew the seam towards the stem. Place the acorn inside the cup and sew in place.

## MATERIALS
→ Small amounts of DK (light worsted/8-ply) yarn in brown and yellow
→ Toy filling

## NEEDLES AND NOTIONS
→ 3mm (US 2 or 3, UK 11) DPN
→ Darning needle

# TEMPLATES

BIRDHOUSE

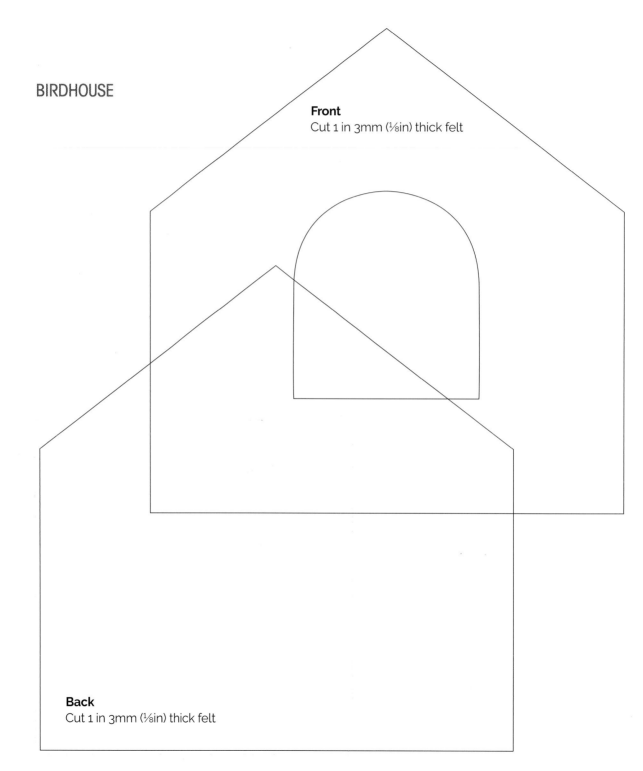

**Front**
Cut 1 in 3mm (⅛in) thick felt

**Back**
Cut 1 in 3mm (⅛in) thick felt

**Base**
Cut 1 in 3mm (⅛in) thick felt

**Side**
Cut 2 in 3mm (⅛in) thick felt

**Roof**
Cut 2 in 3mm (⅛in) thick felt

## CLOUDS

**Small and large clouds**
Cut out what you require
for your hanging hoop

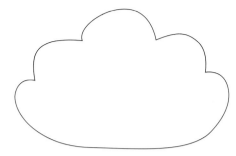

## PEBBLES

**Small pebble**
Cut 2 in felt
(includes 5mm/¼in SA)

**Large pebble**
Cut 2 in felt
(includes 5mm/¼in SA)

**Mistletoe**
Cut 1 in green felt

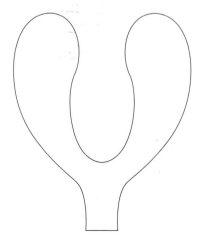

# LEAVES

Draw leaves on felt and stitch before cutting out

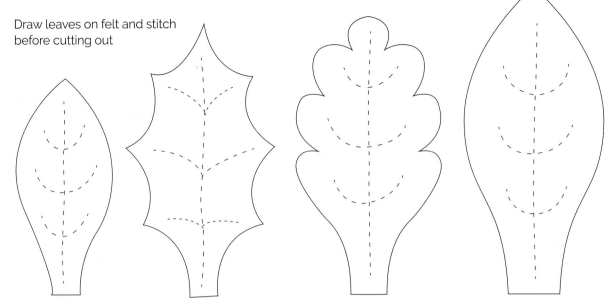

# FLOWERS

**Tropical flower sepals**
Cut 1 in green felt

**Tropical flower outer petals**
Cut 5 in pink felt
(stitch over the
dotted lines)

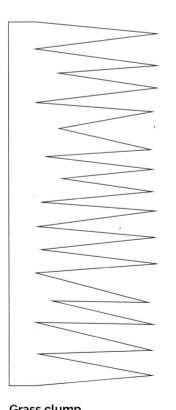

**Grass clump**
Cut 1 in green felt

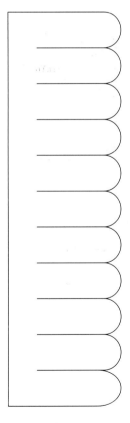

**Tropical flower inner petals**
Cut 1 in orange felt

# INDEX

# DEDICATION

This book is dedicated to all those people without whom it would not have been possible – my fantastic Knitty Kickstarters:

Debbie Olié, Lucy Palmer, Chris Costello, Caroline Silk, Karen Littleton, Helen Allen, Carrie Grayson, Stephanie Wischhusen, Ann Goodman, Phyl Christmas, Janine Foster, Ellie Poore, Caroline Harris, Lisa Shoemaker, Marybeth O'Flynn, Sarah Miller, Sarah Burrough, Frances Webster, Jacqui Turner, Clare Hucknall, Lucy Dolbear, Bonnie Morgan, Bekky Bush, Geri Roberts, Susan Mullen, Connie Taylor, Caroline Turner, Denise Davis, Elizabeth Hamilton-Pearce, Katie Bayliss, Fiona Starkey, Katja Hoebe, Claire Carpenter, Lesley Entecott, Maxine Curtis, Rachel Coopey, Nicola Pawsey, Rachel Clark, Andree Drakeford, Manuela Hirsch, Jane Acott, Helen Benton, Mary Wishart, Jo Webster-Green, Diane Barford, Helen Ketteridge, Penny Last, Sue Jennings, Clare Edgar, Monica Timms, Hilary Coppen, Suzi Daniels, Jo Warwick, Jennifer Aves, Karen Flint, Lucy Horn, Gina Chesher, Ann Axon, Avril Best, Lynne Windeatt, Samantha Molloy, Elizabeth Evatt, Paulina Rogala, Carol Martin, Glynis Lake, Rob Woodcock, Jane Barton, Charlotte Kendrick, Roman Protsiuk, Catherine Fitzgerald, Selina Betts, Margaret Curtis, Jennifer Mohr, Annette Hicks, Ana Dugdale, Michelle Besant, Laura Nicholls, Sharon Gebhard, Nicola Heard, Charlotte Hanlon, Jan Watson, Lorraine Pearson, Gemma Lale, Linda Sylvia Moore, Amy Lipkowitz, Susan Evans, Jane Hobson, Christine Le Cornu, Julia, Katy Heath, Gillian Woodward, Vicky Barrett, Craig de Souza, Karen Parkin, Beryl West, Sarah Waters, Linda Bennett, Eärendil Enbuske, Roz Peel, Colleen Lahey, Mary Schwarz, Sara Levene, Melissa Hellman, Storkstand LLC, Georgy Holden, Iris Rowbotham, Kat Petersen, Brenna Farmer, Marcelle Porteous, Kristen, Penny Miles, Karen Schuiltheis, Chris Gravell, Sharon Grimshaw, Yvonne Dommershuijzen, Lisa Wales, Beverley Stott, Valerie Miller, Judith Ward, Wendie Teesdale, Alison Skelton, Amanda Jeffries, Natalie McLeod, Megan Pugh, Jenny Higgins, Sophie Robertson, Helen Ashton, Lucy Clare, Jenny Steel, Gill Whitehouse, Kate Shurety, Kathleen Martin, Valerie Amonick, Sharon Hammond, Betty Wood, Erika Knight, Bella Harris, Eileen Froggatt, Carter Grondahl, Amanda Inglis, Brett Merritt, Katy Williamson